How to Eat Out in Russia

How to understand the menu and make yourself understood

Dictionary and Phrase Book for the Restaurant

GREMESE

Originally published as:
La Russia al Ristorante

English translation:
Elizabeth Harrowell

Cover design:
Carlo Soldatini

Photocomposition:
Graphic Art 6 s.r.l. – Rome

Printed and bound by:
SO.GRA.TE. – Città di Castello (Italy)

ISBN 88-7301-103-9

And sturgeon, sturgeon on a silver dish?
M. Bulgakov, *The Master and Margarita*

Why?

Why take a guide to the delights of the table with you when you go to Russia? Because, though most people do not realize it, this cuisine is enough to send you into raptures. Totally unknown, Russian cookery is a treasure trove of flavors and surprises. A treasure that we have squeezed and condensed into a pocket guide which never preaches, but explains and advises. An essential traveling companion to help you understand every menu, to tempt your imagination before your palate confirms the experience.
Why – without this book, won't we be able to eat? Well, so as not to get palmed off with just any dish, as ofter happens to tourists abroad, so as to avoid being given whatever is hanging fire in the kitchens because nobody else has ordered it. But above all, because you are curious, the idea of discovering for yourself a tasty, mysterious world attracts the epicurean in you, always ready to have a go.
Why right now? Why didn't you produce your little book ten years ago? Because right now Russia is there to be discovered. Closed cities, secret archives, a market as big as a continent and, above all, the people; for old habits die hard, and the celebrated Russian Soul is still there with its overwhelming fascination. Out of the drawer have come old recipes, dishes quite unproletarian or else simply forgotten or overlooked for half a century. You will share in the singular phenomenon of the resurrection of Russian cuisine – as long as it continues along the right road as it apparently is doing now – or else in its hybridization and colonialization, should imported dishes and Mexican take-aways gain the upper hand.

How to use it?

All you need is a little initiative. Nothing more, and really nothing complicated. It won't take more than five minutes to learn all those strange letters, half-Greek and half-Hottentot. And if you can't even spare that long, you can read the accurate phonetic transcription beside each word and so be sure of expressing exactly what you mean without saying one thing for another – with excellent pronunciation, what's more. Or as a last resort ("Look here!" "**ищи это**", *ishee eta*) you can show the book to the waiter who is generally extremely quick or extremely kind and understanding, and will be able to show you what one thing is, or what kind of filling another one has, in English. On the other hand, if you have already digested the alphabet without difficulty, go straight to the dictionary at the end of the book.

If you notice a word lacking adequate culinary background, like "radish" or "black pepper" or even "tap," you will find the translation right there. If, on the other hand, you require illumination regarding a dish or a particular food or anything else needing further illustration, you will find a reference to one of the sections and to a specific page. The sections on single subjects are at the beginning of the book; you can give them a quick glance or revert to them for detailed information that might prove necessary on the spot.

If you require a clean fork, some salt, or if you feel absolutely obliged to ask a Siberian restaurant-owner for some lamb, all you have to do is to look up the English-Russian dictionary of essential terms.

In the central pages you will find detailed recipes of those dishes which have touched your heart, and should they be at least approximately imitable with the ingredients available at home, you will be able to celebrate next Christmas dinner, for instance, with **щи** (*shee*).

Russian cooking: lard and caviar?

That, in one sense, is correct: sumptuous, refined, but at the same time nutritious and filling. But only if one must at all costs find a common denominator for a cuisine which is eclectic by nature, extremely original, varied and complete because it has undergone a whole series of different influences over the centuries: some remote, such as that of the Mongols, others relatively recent, such as those of the Poles, Germans, French, right through to another Eastern influence, highly noticeable, that of the Caucasian and Asiatic countries annexed in the nineteenth century and recently returned to independence. There is, however, no doubt that the Slav tradition prevails and is as deeply rooted as the Mediterranean tradition in southern Europe. The old-time flavor is very evident in the first-course dishes, soups in nearly all cases, which are complete meals in themselves, with a broth base and never-failing meats, peas, beans and greens. Many of the desserts and the countless fritters and cakes carry in them the memories of celebrations and local festivities which died out centuries ago. As you have gathered, keeping an eye on calories has no part in such an imaginative style of cookery: animal fats are abundantly used, not only for frying but also in flavoring soups, and are more common than butter, while oil, whether seed-oil or sunflower oil, is very secondary. This does not mean that it is unadvisable, even for ten days at a time, to give yourself over, body and soul, to the whole range of Russian dishes including the fattiest and most highly flavored. Noteworthy in this connection is the wide choice of dumplings with a variety of fillings, the frequent use of sour cream and sauces with broth and flour, a preference for elaborate dishes, boiled meat and stews rather than roast and grilled meat. Fish, salted or smoked, is not only the eminent hero of aristocratic starters, but thanks to the recent transformation in the catering world in Russia, it is also regaining its traditional role as a main course (noteworthy are the recipes with stuffed fish) and in soups. Carp, trout, pike and many other freshwater fish are generally used, despite the chronic difficulties in transport and distribution which have limited access to the markets since the Soviet era and which have not yet been completely resolved. The use of spices, anything but sparing in some dishes, is limited to specialties of oriental origins, while in typically Russian cookery the onion is all-important, together with garlic, parsley and herbs less common to us like dill and parsnip. The use of raisins, apples or prunes to give the main course a sweet-and-sour flavor is special though not very widespread. Puddings should really be considered separately from desserts because the pastries and pies (which we have intentionally grouped together under "Floury Fantasies") are as rich and varied as sweets and cakes are little developed; excepting a few pleasant surprises, they are mainly uninteresting and heavy.

Stop after the starters?

This is often unavoidable because the sequence of courses in a Russian meal, particularly on special occasions, follows rites and rhythms quite imponderable for us, whether at a full meal in a high-class restaurant, or at any kind of celebration or party, or even a simple invitation to a private home. Three or four different salad dishes are immediately presented which would be on a par with as many quick meals in a snack bar in the West; while at the same time caviar makes its appearance always accompanied by bread, and a whole series of hors-d'oeuvres, or starters, of fish, cold cuts and sliced meats; without counting fresh vegetables, other "nibbles" and tasty black bread. Then the timing: the starters are still there, nobody changes the plates, mouthful follows mouthful until the dishes are gradually emptied and you are quite convinced that the meal is over. And this is when the soup with croutons and savory pastry and more bread arrive, often fresh out of the oven. Then there is a momentary pause, and the meat or fish course arrives, with plenty of vegetables, and all is lost. The sequence of a Russian meal can be described thus: an initial visual impact, highly dramatic, of the starters nudging each other all over the table rather like the effect made by the main courses of a Chinese meal served at the same time. A slow movement, long and intense; then rather unexpectedly in two brief flourishes, one after the other, the soup course and main course, then of course, the dessert which is normally – and luckily – of short duration. By comparison, even a ten-course banquet in the West is a slow crescendo, your digestion is tested progressively, you can feel how much more you can take, you can choose at your own discretion. A Russian meal leaves no way out, and now that you know why, you realize that there is no defence – and no wish to be defended.

Where to go?

Not to the hotel restaurant, regardless of how many stars it has, so as not to ruin the palate with boring banalities concocted clumsily with an eye to the West. Ideally, go as far as possible from the big cities to where flavors are as authentic and genuine as they once were fifty years ago. Should the intention be to follow a purely gastronomic itinerary, by all means combine it with one of the world's most fascinating journeys, towards the endless reaches of Russia untrodden by tourist's foot, along the country roads,

through the woods and across the steppes up to the far North, or else along the Volga and the Don to Ukraine, to the Caspian Sea and the Black Sea.
Naturally a Russian restaurant in the town will also hold a number of surprises. Traditionally it may resemble a dance-hall with table-service: a large hall, unpretentiously and somewhat anonymously furnished, with the many tables widely spaced to allow people to dance or to move back and forth to the dancing area in front of the small orchestra. The latter plays all kinds of music nearly every evening, from "Kalinka" and "Moscow Nights" to more recent Russian pop and rock, right up to the international standards like those of the Beatles and Tina Turner spiced with daring diction and linguistic acrobatics. After the first bottle of vodka those present let themselves be carried away by the music irrespective of age or figure: a picturesque hully-gully breaks out and finishes in a shower of applause. We can almost hear you muttering "kitsch," and no one will blame you, but wait till you have tried it yourself! The program may have a price, a point made not very clearly on the back of the menu or on a separate note. This particular kind of fixed charge – it generally runs to ten dollars or so – is uncommon for just musical entertainment but it is the rule when hips and bare breasts appear on the stage; this has lately become quite the thing in the same places and on alternate nights to the dance-band. Don't be shocked if nobody seems to notice, nor does the atmosphere change and no one will try to bother you. Apart from the strip-tease, however, it is easy to meet people, especially for men or women who are traveling alone.
Many of the recently opened places are noticeably different from the restaurant-dance halls of the Soviet period, presenting a more intimate, even élitist, atmosphere. The dining space is smaller, sometimes containing only ten tables or so, the furnishings are carefully chosen, tending towards

the pretentious and verging on bad taste (red curtains, stucco), but they do show creativity in spite of the limited means available. Frescos, large flower arrangements, aquariums, columns and separate cubicles, often candles and low lights; there may be chamber music, or piano bar-style music or none at all.
So far we have been talking only about proper restaurants (**ресторан**, *restaran*) but there are many alternatives starting from the **кафе** (*cafe*), places not necessarily smaller but more popular during the day than in the evening, without any sort of entertainment, a limited choice of food, prices fairly low, in general, and a lower standard of service. The **кафе**, which normally serve only complete meals, are giving way to places for quicker snacks providing hot dishes and somewhere to sit but these are on a smaller scale with a self-service counter (**бистро**, *bistro*), or else are more refined with a brief, highly specialized menu.
You may even have the rather doubtful privilege of being among the last customers of a **рюмочная** (*ryoomaknaya*) or of a **столовая** (*stalovaya*), small dives on the way to extinction featuring nameless smells, where your watery coffee is ladled out of a bucket, and marble eggs and plastic chicken decorate the windows. Here you will find vodka, beer and three or four round legless tables suspended chairless three feet above the floor in cavelike darkness conducive to philosophical meditation.
The beer-houses, once similarly smoke-filled and closed have all become **пуб** (pubs) or **пивная** (*pivnaya*) looking more attractive, complete with Western beers and sometimes German-style food.
The **казино** (*kazeeno*) and the exclusive **найт-клуб** *(nah-eet kloop)* go beyond gastronomic pleasures since, of late, the attractions of St. Petersburg and Moscow nights appear irresistible.

AND SOME WISE PRACTICAL TIPS?

Let's start from the last point mentioned. Like saloons in the Far West or Chicago in the thirties, everything has already been said about the Russia of the New Rich and the New Mafia, with and without exaggeration. Caution is necessary and the advice of friends or tour operators regarding the choice of eating places can be truly valuable, but unnecessary alarm does not make for good digestion nor a good trip! Some problems are more immediate and practical than the likelihood of finding oneself in the midst of a shoot-out: prices, for example. They are occasionally outrageous. Russians eat out to make an impression, to certify their achievement of social status and more or less to paint the town red. With a different end in mind, it is quite possible to enjoy a good meal without squeezing credit cards dry. A few simple precautions are enough, starting with the question **можно посмотреть меню?** (*mozhna pasmatryet' minyoo*) "Can you show me the menu?" although for the most part it is displayed outside or at the entrance. Prices may be shown in dollars (to avoid having to keep up with inflation) or in roubles, but payment will always be in roubles so do make sure that the current exchange rate has been correctly applied. Bearing in mind that the price/quality ratio is much more variable than elsewhere in the world, it is still well worth taking the chance of an evening out in one of the new, high-class restaurants, although most of our advice runs in favor of the middle-to-high-level places. These include almost all restaurants in Russia, seeing that the laws of competition have not yet been sufficiently absorbed and no one has as yet tapped the endless potentialities of low-cost catering for such a vast market.
A complete meal can cost from around $25 to $50 per person, of which at least a third is for wines, especially

imported, and spirits which may be exorbitantly priced. On the other hand, you will save if you can adjust to, and risk, dining on vodka. The first courses are inexpensive and should all be tasted; a rule to be broken is that laid down by hotels and organized groups, ordaining that they be ordered only at lunch time. The main courses are more expensive as they are always large helpings and include vegetables. The biggest items on the bill are inevitably the starters, at least two or an assortment being necessary for anything substantial. However, it would be an unforgivable sacrilege to omit them.

During the first years of the *perestroyka* there was an unpleasant trick in use of distracting the customer with small talk and, occasionally without even consulting him, serving the complete assortment: ten or fifteen items on the menu, including the sardines. Such irritating ploys of waiters or restaurant owners are now luckily very rare, since the fully booked era has now passed. Then, bookings had to be made two weeks beforehand, and tips and countertips were the only ways of ensuring the appearance of a free table at the last minute.

Reservations are necessary only for the evening and only for some places. Beware, when you do reserve or when you are just sitting down, of the question: **накрыть на стол?** (*nakreet nastol*) "Do we set for a complete meal?"). Post-Soviet catering, now almost entirely privatized, furnishes service in constant improvement, of course not always and not everywhere, but on occasion of a very high quality. It should not be forgotten that the Russian waiter of the past was a sort of jack-of-all-trades, money-exchanger, vendor of caviar and amber, a "consultant" ready to solve any kind of problem for the tourist. He had initiative, intelligence and a working knowledge of several languages and, considering the specific circumstances, he possessed tact and presence of

mind. His successors (for in the main he has now made his fortune) are just as friendly and talkative, briefed on the rules of "polite society" and will no doubt be able to help you in any situation.
Russian restaurants are almost always open from 12 noon to 12 midnight except for an hour in the afternoons though this is not a general rule. Closing time may be 10 or 11 P.M. in winter and is in any case very elastic; some places even stay open all night. Generally there is no service charge. There are no tourist menus nor, fortunately, any tourist restaurants. Credit cards are not accepted everywhere, hardly anywhere outside the big cities. One last tip for tea tottlers: you may have trouble both in hotels where the drinking water is brownish (but effectively drinkable) and at restaurants where all local mineral waters are so rich in minerals as to be undrinkable. Some years ago this was a serious problem, but today one can fall back on soft drinks.

Sophisticated and varied, characteristic and aristocratic, the flavor of the different types of salmon and sturgeon and their highly rated eggs reflects the real Russia, culinary and otherwise. It may or may not please – it usually does – but it never leaves the visitor indifferent. It is not by chance that a typical Russian meal commences with the giddy acceleration of the starters: everything all at once, the best at once, so these fish that are excellent boiled or baked are almost always used salted or smoked to be served cold at a moment's notice with magnificent effect. Salmon and sturgeon in our part of the world may be quite unknown, but both come of a numerous family full of delicious surprises. By salmon we mean the Pacific salmon which does not swim back up the rapids like its Atlantic cousin, but reproduces once only, then dies. There are several species, such as the dog salmon (**кета**, *keeta*), the hunchback salmon (**горбуша**, *garboosha*), the red salmon (**нерка**, *nyerka*) and the impressive royal salmon (**чавыча**, *chaveecha*), weighing up to twenty-five kilos. Even more majestic and singular are the sturgeon, all of them long in shape with pointed head and bony projections along the back. The most common is the Russian sturgeon (**осётр**, *asyotr*) to be found both in the Caspian Sea and in many inland rivers, but it is neither the biggest nor the best. The crown belongs indubitably to the beluga (**белуга**, *bilooga*) which reaches nine meters in length and over a ton in weight: the bigger it is, the more tender and tasty is its highly prized flesh. Another sought-after kind is the sevruga (**севрюга**, *sivryooga*) while the sterlet (**стерлядь**, *stirlyat*), the smallest of the sturgeon, is a freshwater fish only. Locally many other fish, salted or smoked, are used in starters and are listed in the Russian-English dictionary at the back of this guide. Herrings, sardines and mackerel are held in greater esteem than in our part of the world and should not be disdained, particularly the little anchovies served with sunflower oil and chives.

Балык (*baleek*) the general name used commercially to indicate the dorsal part – the best – of salmon and sturgeon. It is served among the starters, generally smoked, and the menu will indicate from what type of fish it comes, e.g. **балык осетровый** (*baleek* from Russian sturgeon).

Блины с икрой (*blinee sikroy*): one of the great traditional dishes used abroad in restaurants famous for their international cuisine, in Russia it has always been considered for the elite. The **блины** (see "Floury Fantasies") are served on a hot plate with one dish of butter and another heaped with black caviar which is to be spread on each one.

Бок осетровый (*bok asitrovyi*): a long strip of flesh from the side of sturgeon served smoked as a starter; only from the larger varieties, the beluga in particular.

Горбуша (*garboosha*): the humpback salmon with pink flesh is used in starters both smoked and salted.

Икра (*ikra*): caviar. Two million eggs. That is the average number found in the ovary sacs of a female sturgeon caught in the Volga delta. Freed from the membrane and sieved to separate the mass, they are then salted and tinned to produce the supreme delicacy: caviar! In Russia only caviar from sturgeon and salmon is commercialized and used for culinary purposes although eggs from other fish are used in small local industries. These are also called caviar and are on sale in the West. The preparation of caviar is very simple, basically two types: **икра зернистая** (*ikra zerneestaya*) by far the more common, in whole grains easily separable one

from the other; and **икра паюсная** (*ikra payooznaya*) with crushed grains which look more compact and unseparated: nutritionally of greater value but less highly esteemed and now little commercialized.
Caviar is also classified according to the salt content; the lower it is, the fresher and more delicate the product (and the less it will keep). The caviar with the lowest salt content (2-3%) will be in a tin marked **малосольная** (*malassol'naya*) or MALOSSOL on export products. The caviar industry is for the time being still a state monopoly so the airtight tins (generally 100 g or 90 g) are easily identifiable: blue tins for black caviar and green tins for red caviar; or jars with screw-tops. The latter are advisable because close inspection – the grains must not appear dry – ensures against acquiring a counterfeit product. Once unobtainable, caviar is now available everywhere at ridiculously low prices compared to those abroad: the distribution channels are however inscrutable, so don't be too annoyed if your long-awaited caviar should have a sticky taste... of plastic. Always check the "Best by" date on the container, and buy preferably in shops rather than from roadside stalls. If you should chance to pass through Astrakan, the main production center of black caviar, have no scruples about buying under-the-counter kilo or half-kilo tins of exceptional caviar, "homemade" or purloined at its freshest from the factory.

Икра осетровая (*ikra asitrovaya*) is the caviar *par excellence*, the black caviar obtained mainly from the sturgeon which travel up the Volga from the Caspian Sea. The grains are very delicate, from dark gray to brown with a green tinge – this last is excellent. Eggs from the various types of sturgeon are not sold separately according to type, but those of beluga can be identified by their larger size (2-3 mm. or, about 1/8 in.) from those of stellate sturgeon or sterlet

(1-1.5 mm. or, about 1/16 in.). Restaurant portions are of approximately 30 g and always come with butter and white bread.

Икра кетовая (*ikra kitovaya*): red caviar comes from several varieties of Pacific salmon and is generally larger in diameter (about 3 mm. or, about 1/8 in.) and its flavor is slightly more bitter than that of black caviar. The outside membrane is tougher so you get the strange but pleasant sensation of actually feeling the grains burst in your mouth. The most common type in commerce is that of the Siberian salmon (**кета**, *keta*) of a pearly pink color, but all the salmon family caviar is canned under the same name; that from the humpback salmon is smaller, pink with touches of yellow, while royal salmon caviar is a dark red, almost verging on purple.

Крабы (*krabi*): the enormous Pacifc crabs reaching up to seven kilos in weight give excellent meat, white and compact, extremely tasty and widely used in salads, can also be served as a separate starter.

Лосось (*lasos*): the most common and least costly of the salmon family; it is from the Caspian Sea and in general is not salted for a starter. It is very good canned and is found in all shops at a low price; hence it is frequently used in home cooking, above all in salads.

Осетрина (*azitreena*): the flesh of the Russian sturgeon, but also of the other fish of the same family, served as a starter or in gelatine. It is marble white, delicate and totally boneless.

Раки натуральные (*raki naturalnyi*): a typical beerhouse dish (**пивная** *pivnaya*) where it is traditionally eaten with beer. The large river crayfish, boiled and chilled, are served with the carrots, onions and herbs of the broth in which they were cooked.

Рыбное ассорти (*reebnaya assortee* – mixed fish): it is the most common fish starter, therefore it is recommended for the "first evening" as an introduction to the most attractive specialties; in any case it is always a good choice in those restaurants whose menu is not so varied. Generally it includes caviar, red and black, one variety of smoked sturgeon and one of salmon, usually salted. According to the locality, other freshwater fish will be added, or else little anchovies, all served with butter and parsley. The quantity varies but is generally plentiful.

Сёмга (*syomga*): it is the salmon of the Arctic Sea and the White Sea and is caught in the rivers of the far North. The meat, light red with shades of pink, is that of the salmon family most sought-after for starters. Lightly salted (6% approx.), it is commonly used also in bars for sandwich fillings.

Сиг (*seek*): this freshwater fish of the salmon family is delicious and much in demand and is present in small quantities in the West in the variety called whitefish. As a starter it is served smoked but unfortunately it is rarely to be found in restaurants. Its tender pink caviar is only to be acquired by traveling through inland Russia, directly from the fishermen.

Тёша (*tyosha*): this is the side section of sturgeon and salmon, a wide, thin strip of flesh, oily and very tasty. As a starter it is used both salted and smoked but it is not very common.

Яйца фаршированные икрой (*yaitsa farshirovanyi ikroy* – eggs stuffed with caviar): eating caviar by the spoonful was the prerogative of wealthy nineteenth-century grain merchants in Russia. Actually that is not the ideal way, as the flavor of caviar is so strong that to eat it at its best requires bread and butter as is most usual, or else hard-boiled eggs: the yolks are removed and they are filled with caviar, almost always the red variety.

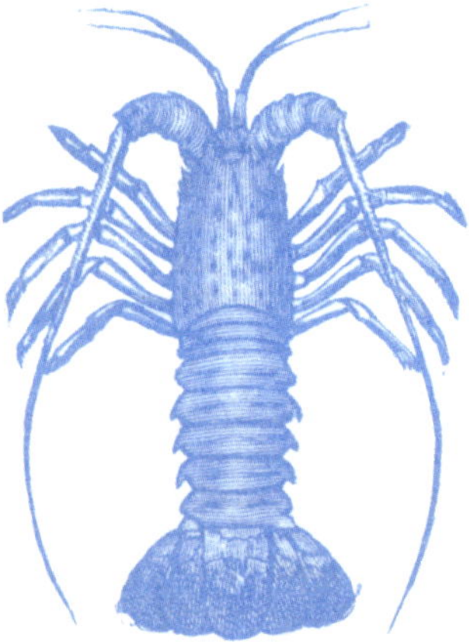

Although Russian preserved meats have not made a name for themselves internationally, there is a good variety and a selection of unusual flavors. Cooked and smoked varieties are more common than the uncooked ones; they are highly spiced but generally not hot.
Lard is commonly used, as are lower-quality meats which, however, do not lack flavor. The most common is without doubt **колбаса** (*kalbasa*) a sausage of pork and beef, mainly cooked, minced and mixed with the fat. Its preparation is varied and flavor ranges from salami to mortadella; so we will offer a separate list of the various types.
A continental hotel breakfast can be the occasion to taste some of the best. Restaurants, on the other hand, provide them separately only as starters while they are served more commonly in the **мясное ассорти** (*myaznoy assortee*, see "National Dishes"). They are also used in tasty, hot salads.
To obtain the widest possible choice, we advise you to drop into a **гастроном** (*gastronom*), the Russian supermarket; remember, however, that these products will not be sliced for you, either by hand or by machine.

Ветчина (*vitchina*): this is a **окорок** (see below), a boned, pressed sausage, smaller in size, with less fat and of excellent quality.

Ветчино-рубленая колбаса (*vitchina-rooblyenaya kalbasa*): a ham-like sausage of beef and pork. The meats are finely minced, deep pink, and flavored with garlic.

Грудинка (*groodeenka*): smoked sausage made from the underside of the pig, rather fat; it is used as a starter and in first courses.

Докторская колбаса (*doktarskaya kalbasa*): made from

cooked beef and pork, eggs and powdered milk. It is homogeneous and totally fat-free, flavored with cardamom.

Карбонад (*karbanat*) : roast pork fillet, very lean and delicate.

Ливерная колбаса (*leevirnaya kalbasa*): a thin sausage, from lower-quality beef and pork and offal such as liver and lung with the addition of eggs and flour. There are several types, the best of which are soft enough to spread on bread, gray-pink in color, seasoned with onion, black pepper and ginger. The main flavor is that of liver.

Любительская колбаса (*lyoobeetilskaya kalbasa*): cooked sausage of first-class cuts of beef and pork, seasoned with black pepper and nutmeg. Pink in color with small lumps of fat, it has a delicate, spicy flavor.

Московская колбаса (*maskovskaya kalbasa*): a raw, smoked sausage of beef and pork. The meats are not finely minced; it is hot, flavored with black pepper and nutmeg.

Окорок (*okarak*): from the leg of the pig, similar to our cooked ham, deep pink with a narrow veining and outer layer of fat. It may also be smoked. The best known is that from Tambov (**тамбовский окорок**, *tambovsky okarak*).

Полтавская колбаса (*paltavskaya kalbasa*): lightly smoked, a mixture of beef and pork, it is rather salty, hot and spicy, flavored with garlic.

Сервелат (*servelat*): smoked beef and pork sausage, rather chunky, slightly hot. It is one of the most popular and widespread of the preserved meats and is similar to Italian salami.

In all the wide variety and specialties of Russian cookery, cheeses by and large take a secondary role. Neither by culture nor by tradition do they come to the fore. They are often eaten between meals and above all at breakfast; but they never appear before dessert. They may not be available in all restaurants, and even if they do appear, they will be among the starters under the laconical heading **сыр** *(sir)*, which doesn't specify the kind of cheese, the assortment being in general extremely limited. The choice of **сырное ассорти** (*sirnai asartee* – mixed cheeses) will, we fear, have to await the next edition of this guide.
The Russian dairy industry went through a serious production crisis in the eighties; as a consequence, for a long time the only cheese available was a poor-quality type of **российский сыр** (*raseeskee sir*), a hybrid combined with other cheeses missing at that time. At the present time very many foreign cheeses in fact monopolize the market, but nearly all the traditional Russian cheeses are available, of which we here give a brief description. We have not included some products which are in fact no more than the Russian version of famous foreign cheeses, as **швейцарский сыр** (*shveetsarskee sir* – Swiss gruyère), **чеддар** (cheddar), **рокфор** (Roquefort).
One tip: it is really worth trying the Russian butter, with a higher fat content than ours but also much tastier.

Алтайский сыр (*altaiskee sir*): produced in the Altay mountain region with cow's milk from high pastures, it is a particularly tasty cheese with a characteristic aftertaste of hazelnuts. A fairly hard cheese featuring small oval holes, it is not easily found outside the production area.

Брынзд (*brintsa*): a typical cheese from the Caucasian Republics, widespread all over Russia. It is left to season in brine which gives it a very particular flavor, decidedly salty and acidulate. Rindless, white, of medium consistency, it is produced mainly from sheep's milk.

Волжский сыр (*volshskee sir*): a piquant cheese with a strong smell, soft in consistency with holes of irregular shape and distribution.

Голландский сыр (*galandski sir*): this is the Russian version of Dutch gruyère but with a stronger slightly acidulate flavor. Resilient in consistency, with circular holes, light yellow in color.

Домашний сыр (*damashnee sir*): a fermented cheese with a particular acidulous taste, creamy with hardly any salt, white or off-white in color. It is generally eaten with fruit or vegetables.

Российский сыр (*rsseeskee sir*): a semi-hard cheese, bright yellow, tasty, it is the most widely commercialized cheese in Russia.

Творог (*tvorak*): a creamy fresh cheese similar to ricotta cheese but slightly fattier. Often eaten together with **сметана** (*smitana*, see "The Basics") or with sugar. It is used in the preparation of many dishes like **вареники** (*varyeniki*, see "Dishes from ex-USSR countries") and **сырники** (*sirniki*, see "Floury Fantasies"). One kind, with raisins, is especially suitable with sweets.

Углический сыр (*oogleecheskee sir*): a half-fat cheese, not fully seasoned and slightly piquant, an elastic consistency, light yellow, with round holes.

One of the recurring pictures that come to mind through literary or other allusions to nineteenth-century Russia is that of ovens, loaded bakery shelves, and cellar rooms whence issue delicious fragrances. Further, smoky taverns where golden, crusty rolls unfailingly accompany the vodka, endless wheatfields stretching across the world's one-time greatest storehouse, the fabulous black earth, all these speak of a land where flour and bread-making has a tradition dating back centuries, a daily rite and a perfect commercial machine. The Soviet bread industry expanded and standardized this whole sector as well, but the importance of bread products has not decreased although both industrial and household production have changed notably. Nowadays old recipes are being rediscovered, the inventiveness of the small artisans is flourishing and, as a result, there is an increase in variety of production. Cakes, buns, savoury rolls and toasted specialties subject the tourist to constant, delicious temptation. One surprising feature of many of these delicacies is that they can be filled or served with either sweet or savoury foods and are eaten both during and at the end of the meal. Although there are not many different types of bread itself, either in shape or baking method, the quality and the flavor are excellent, especially the rye bread. White bread is sold in French bread shape (**батон**, *baton*), brown in rectangular loaves (**буханка**, *bookhanka*), while the roll (**булочка**, *boolachka*) is generally like a large lozenge. Many restaurants bake their own bread; it is always served hot.

Блины (*blinee*): these pancakes, round and hot, were the symbols of the return of the sun in spring during the frenetic Russian Carnival celebrations in the Middle Ages. They are still always present on special occasions and in every restaurant of any standing: golden and slightly crisp, always soft and delicate, of dark yellow tending towards tan, small and thicker than crêpes though never thicker than 3 millimeters (or, 1/8 in.). The secret of *blinee* is in the pan which must be cast iron and in the special flour. They may be eaten as starters or as desserts according to what they are served with: caviar, sturgeon, salmon or else jam or fruit such as currants and berries. They come to table on a hot dish, piled one on the other, unfailingly accompanied by **сметана** (*smitana*, see "The Basics").

Ватрушки (*vatrooshkee*): small baked buns, round and flat, with jam, cottage cheese or apples.

Гренки (*gryenkyi*): toasted white bread, spread with butter or cheese and put in the oven till golden brown and crisp.

Калач (*kalach*): a round roll, with a curving braid worked along one side to look something like a woman's purse. Crusty and golden outside, very soft inside.

Кокурок (*kakoorok*): a roll with egg and cheese filling.

Крендель (*kryendil*): a rather large loaf made, in fact, of two **калач** (*kalach*, see above) baked together like a capital *B* or, turned through 90° like a heart.

Кулебяка (*koolibyaka*): one of the most famous Russian specialties though it is generally made in the home and unusual in restaurants. It is a long, narrow, thick pastry with plenty of rich filling, or even with three different kinds. The most common is of minced meat, rice and hard-boiled eggs, in three layers inside tasty pastry. Fish fillings are also excellent: whitefish, well known but a great rarity, turbot, pike, cod.

Кулич (*koolik*): a traditional Easter cake, conical in shape, of varying sizes; once upon a time they were baked as big as buckets in convents. They are generally homemade, of a simple soft mixture, to which are added hazelnuts, raisins and candied fruit. The old tradition of taking them to be blessed in church at Easter together with the colored eggs is once again in use.

Оладьи (*aladi*) pancakes which differ from **блины** (*blinee*, see above) in that the mixture is more compact and also because it is often prepared with a vegetable purée, for example zucchini or pumpkin as a base, or else with pieces of apple.

Пирог (*pirok*) a traditional holiday dish, it is a pie with a filling of meat or liver, fish, cabbage, mushrooms, rice with hard-boiled eggs. The shape varies, rectangular or triangular, or a particular shape for a particular celebration, maybe decorated with pastry trees, stars or circles. It is baked in the oven and is usually quite deep. The sweet **пирог** is totally different, filled with jam, fresh fruit or ricotta cheese, similar to our pies and tarts.

Пирожки (*pirashkee*): savoury pastries, baked or fried. They come in all shapes, some mouthful-sized, others the size of a bread roll. The filling can be savoury (meat, fish, mushrooms, rice) or sweet (cottage cheese, jam).

Пончики (*ponchiki*): fried doughnuts, soft and fairly big. If they are ball-shaped they will contain jam or apple. Being fried, they may not be the lightest specialty to choose, but served hot they are delicious.

Пряники (*pryaniki*): small cakes of unleavened dough with sugar, honey and molasses, almost fat-free, characterized by an intense fragrance of spices: cinnamon, cloves, pepper, nutmeg, cardamom, ginger. The mixture is compact but not hard. They come in different shapes and sizes, generally round, with a geometrical pattern on the top crust, golden brown and shiny with eggwhite. There is also one kind flavored with mint.

Расстегай (*rastigai*): these are a particular type of **пирожки** (*pirashkee*, see above), molded into a boat shape with a characteristic opening left on the upper side. If the filling is fish, as it usually is, a piece of smoked sturgeon or salmon will be put in the opening; or if it has a meat filling, chopped hard-boiled egg, and pickled mushrooms, for a plain mushroom filling. They are often served with soups, with hot broth poured into the famous opening.

Сухари (*sookharee*): slightly sweetened dry crouton-style biscuits, crisp and crunchy, eaten with tea or with jam or honey. Some are on the market with poppy seeds or raisins. The same name **сухари** is given to homemade croutons of toasted brown bread to be eaten mainly with soups.

Сырники (*sirniki*): small rolls of cottage cheese mixed with flour and egg then fried in breadcrumbs. They are eaten sprinkled with icing sugar together with **сметана** (*smitana*, see "The Basics").

Хачапури (*khachapoori*): a flattish roll, round or square, stuffed with slightly sour cheese. It is a specialty from Georgia but is now very popular all over Russia.

Хворост (*khvorast*): large, rose-shaped pancakes, made with thick, dry and rather sour batter. Spiced occasionally with cinnamon, they are served with icing sugar.

Чебуреки (*cheboory**e**ki*): a sort of salted, fried doughnut, crescent-shaped, stuffed with minced mutton and onion. They are sold on street stalls especially in winter and must be eaten hot.

Or rather, "*the* spirit." Transparent, almost tasteless, very light on the palate, **водка** (*vodka*) is a legend and a rite in Russia from which no one can escape. It is the perfect embodiment of the wild spirit, part masochist and part chaotic; of the Russian sleigh rushing towards the abyss. It has not got a lot in common with our moonlit iced vodka, wistful and pretentiously refined. One drinks as much of it as possible, at whatever temperature it happens to be, with energy, warmth, physical joy, communicativeness, but with a touch of melancholy. As a rule it is drunk during meals, interrupted with ever more frequent and less coherent toasts, at the end of each of which one must down a glassful – and not a small one – in one gulp. It certainly burns like fire on the way down, which is why the Russians follow it up with a gherkin, which may seem extreme, but is most assuredly an excellent fire-extinguisher. A bottle of 75 cl is generally considered enough for three people, which is a lot as it is, but at the end of a successful evening when the foreigner accepts the challenge inevitably offered, that amount can easily double. Beware, even if you are used to drinking: you are playing an away match!
There are a great many kinds, but according to the experts, the one and only real vodka is **Московская особая** (*maskofskaya asobaya*) "Special Moscow Vodka," in the unattractive bottle with a green label and a screw top which has always been for export. And there is also the manufacturer **Кристалл** (*kreestal*) of Moscow, the unopposed leader, whose production of the self-same vodka in the self-same bottles labelled in tiny print is sold for double the price (which, in any case, is not high). They say that the secret lies in the particularly soft water of the rivers of central Russia which is enough to get the upper hand on ferocious competition such as Smirnoff and Keglevich which have been producing vodka for a century but which lack the basic raw material, having left the country. Apart from water

and yeast, the ingredients are grain and rye malt, with a limited number of other cereals. The alcohol proof is fixed at 40°, a number which has acquired a decidedly symbolic meaning in Russian.
Other "pure" vodkas of the same quality as **Московская особая** (*maskofskaya asobaya*) are **Посолская** (*pasolskaya* – "The Ambassador's") and **Золотое кольцо** (*zalatoyay kal'tso*) – "Ring of Gold," produced on a more limited scale, considered luxury vodka and more suitable to give as a gift because of the design of the bottle. This is an aspect in which the many new vodka brands have shown a good deal of imagination in their invasion of the market in recent years; the far-fetched bottle "with a hole in it" of the **Чайковская** (*chaikofskaya* – Tchaikovsky vodka) is one example. Frequently, however, these new brands are produced abroad and are of poor quality. Another very common vodka is **Столичная** (*Stalichnaya* – "of the Capital") of slightly lower quality which contains traces of sugar besides the usual ingredients. The slightly off-center flavor of **Русская** (*rooskaya* – "Russia") is corrected with cinnamon. Decidedly different is **Пшеничная** (*pshenichnaya*), which unlike the others is produced with wheat instead of rye. The traditional Ukrainian vodka, **Горилка** (*khareelka*) is also made from wheat. The alcohol proof of some vodkas has been enhanced up to the 56° of **Охотничая** (*akhotnichaya* – "of the Hunter"), but here we are really talking about a different kind of spirit altogether. The same goes for other so-called vodkas aromatized with plant essences: the **Лимонная** (*limonnaya*), with lemon; the **Перцовка** (*pirtsofka*), with chili; the **Можжевеловая** (*mazhivyelavaya*) with juniper.

Глинтвейн (*glintvyein* – mulled wine): red wine spiced with cloves and nutmeg, sweetened and served hot, with a slice of lemon and a dash of brandy.

Кизлярка (*kislyarka*): distilled from fruit: apples, pears, plums or apricots, in varying combinations, produced in the northern Caucasus and in the Ukraine, in the Stavropol' and Kuban' regions.

Коньяк (*kanyak*): produced in Georgia and Armenia especially, this is an appreciable brandy, aged from at least 7 years up to 12 or 15. The best-known brandies are **Енисели** (*yeniseliee*), **Вардзия** (*varzeeya*) and **Ереван** (*yerivan*).

Крюшон (*kriooshon*): a sweet, refreshing alcoholic drink the basic ingredient of which is either white wine or Russian "champagne" with the addition of brandy, a sweet liqueur like Maraschino, fruit (apricots, peaches or pineapple) and sugar. It is prepared and macerated for a while before serving well-chilled.

Самогон (*samagon*): not infrequently it happens that you think you have gone into the wrong room in a Russian home, quickly shut the door and go to your host to show you the way, only to discover that it was not the wrong door after all: quite often the bathroom has been transformed into a home distillery with coils, stills and all equipment necessary. **Самогон** is a kind of homemade brandy following age-old traditions, corrupted to a certain extent by the taint of alcoholism, but certainly picturesque. Still today in outlying villages large "communal" distilleries exist which the locals use in turns, while hardware shops frequently stock the complete kit for the home now that the "prohibitionism" of the Gorbachov era is over – a good idea for an unusual gift. **Самогон** is known graphically as "superbomb" and occasionally vaunts a most discouraging smell, but in itself it is neither good nor bad; it all depends on the skill of the do-it-yourself distiller (which can be quite amazing) and on the quality of the ingredients. It is made by fermenting food containing starch or sugar: from sugar itself to chocolates, syrups, potatoes or bottled or tinned tomatoes. The best of course are those based on cereals, closely related to vodka, or those made from fruit. **медовуха** (*myedovookha*), a spirit home-distilled from honey, is fantastic and has the unusual feature of producing the effects of its substantial alcoholic content, a good half-hour after it has been imbibed.

Северное сияние (*syevirnaye siyanye*): "northern lights," a name worthy of the most famous of all Russian cocktails made with one part vodka, two parts Russian "champagne."

Тутовка (*tootofka*): brandy produced in Azerbaidjan and Armenia from black or white mulberries. After being distilled it has a typical fragrance which is quite pleasant, with green and yellow shadings.

Чача (*chacha*): Georgia. Distilled from poor-quality unripe grapes and grape stems, with a pleasant fragrance of wine.

In spite of the considerable extent of land devoted to grape growing and the large amount of wine produced in the Soviet period, Russia has always depended on quality wines imported from countries within her sphere of political influence, notably Georgia and Moldavia, both with ancient wine-making traditions; and then, one step behind, Armenia, Azerbaidjan and Uzbekistan. However much wine is held in high consideration and widely drunk, it is still rather a luxury article kept for special occasions and is outside the deeply rooted traditions; of the people. And since wine culture is still unfamiliar, you may find yourself drinking dessert wines with your meal because they are much more common than normal table wines, or else wines from Georgia which are by nature semi-sweet. The latter are noticeably more original than the others on the market in Russia and are characterized by definite variations in proof from one vintage to another. There is no doubt that in shops, and to an even greater degree in restaurants, imported wines take the lion's share although they are decidedly more expensive and their origins are not always absolutely clear. In spite of the recently introduced state monopoly in the sector, the risks of imitations are still high since the intrinsic Russian ingenuity for making ends meet has found expression in decanting, the use of additives, and imaginative corks and labels. By no means be discouraged: there is also a lot of fun in rummaging around small markets outside subway stations, deciphering a babel of writing (now no longer in Cyrillic) and discovering perhaps a rare bottle of famous South African white wine tucked away behind a presumably Italian wine produced in Poland!

Алиготе (*aligotay*): Moldavia. One of the best Moldavian wines, much used at table, coming from the Aligoté vineyards. A dry white wine, straw-yellow with green shades, it has a balanced flavor with a slight fruity bouquet.

Аштарах (*ashtarakh*): Armenia. A famous wine of the Jerez type, produced from the local Voskeat grapes. It has a full, sweet flavor and delicate aroma.

Гурджаани (*gooryaani):* Georgia. A dry white wine of a light golden-yellow color, with a delicate bouquet and a full, harmonious, fresh taste.

Каберне (*kabernay*): Moldovia. The best red wine from Moldavia is a Cabernet derived from Bordeaux grapes: soft, almost velvet, a full taste, intense ruby color with sober bouquet, very fluid. In Russia, Cabernet Abrau is produced in the only really important wine-producing area, Krasnodar.

Кагор (*kagor*): Uzbekistan, Azerbaidjan, Moldavia. A red dessert wine, approximately 16°, a dark ruby red, with a full flavor, very soft, with a hint of raspberry and redcurrant.

Киндзмараули (*kindzmarauli*): Georgia. Red, by nature semi-sweet, produced by local craftsmen from their carefully selected grapes. It is one of the most famous Georgian wines, popular throughout Russia: it is said that is was Stalin's favorite – one of the qualities attributed to him by Regime propaganda was that of being a wine connoisseur.

Кодры (*kodri*): Moldavia. Red with a full flavor, but with delicacy; ruby red with orange highlights, an intense, complex, very fragrant bouquet. In aging, it gains a slight flavor of wild rose.

Лидия молдавская (*leedya maldavskaya*): Moldavia. A rosé liqueur wine of an attractive color made from Isabella grapes, about 16°, a fresh taste, full bouquet with a hint of strawberry.

Мерло (*merlo*): Moldavia. Produced in the micro-climate of Romaneshty, Moldavian Merlot is a dry, balanced wine with a typical, harmonious bouquet, and dark ruby-red color.

Напареули (*napareyooli*): Georgia. White with a pleasant, smooth taste, a vivacious and continuous bouquet, light yellow in color with a tendency towards green.

Петра (*petra*): Georgia. White, excellent balance, lightly palatable, with an original fruity harmonious taste. Light yellow in color, between 9° and 10°.

Променисте (*promenistay*) Ukraine. A table white, light yellow in color, obtained from Italian Riesling wines. Its flavor is dry and fresh.

Псоу (*psou*): Abchazia. A white wine from the Caucasus, sweet with a strong flavor. Light straw-yellow, fresh vivacious taste with a harmonious structure.

Рислинг (*reesling*): among the relatively few quality wines produced in Russia this Riesling Abrau deserves mention; golden yellow with greenish lights, a distinctive subtle bouquet and pleasant taste with a noticeable tartness. Moldavian Riesling, reminiscent of Moselle wines, is of superior quality, fresh and very delicate with a highly characteristic, exquisite fragrance.

Ркацители (*rkatseteli*): Georgia. Dry white table wine, amber in color, more intense than the other Georgian wines, savory and full, with good body. The bouquet has undertones of honey. It is also produced in Moldavia.

Советское шампанское (*savyetskaye shampanskaye*): One place where the Soviet Union still exists is on the labels of the famous "Soviet Champagne," a sparkling wine made with varying grapes and methods, in many of the states of the ex-federation. In any case it is an extremely widespread favorite and no one would dare give up the brand name (except some wineries in the Crimea which are launching new names). It comes in several kinds: brut, semi-dry, sweetish and sweet.

Совиньон (*sovinyon*): The Moldavian kind is made from two types of Sauvignon grape, the yellow and the green; it has a subtle, delicate bouquet and a strong but harmonious flavor. The Sauvignon of Kuban' is one of the best of the Ukrainian wines.

Твиши (*tveeshi*): Georgia. A naturally semi-sweet white wine, 10°-12°, straw-colored tending towards a greeny shade, with a fresh taste and delicate bouquet.

Фетяска (*fityaska*): Moldavia. A very delicate white wine the word **фетяска**, in fact, means "girl." It has a slightly ethereal fragrance, a fine, light flavor. There is also a choice quality with three years aging.

Хванчкара (*khavanchkara*): Georgia. A naturally sweet red produced in the western region of Georgia and much appreciated in Russia, it has a harmonious, pleasantly sweet taste.

Цинандали (*tsinandali*): Georgia. Straw-yellow in color, 10-12°, a rounded, balanced flavor, and delicate fruit-tinged bouquet.

Цымлянское игристое (*tsimlyanskaye igristaye*): Russia. The village of Tsimljanskaja on the Don is the traditional place of production of this most famous of the sparkling wines, well known even before the Revolution.

Чёрный доктор (*chorniy doktar*): Crimea. Literally "black doctor," it is a celebrated dessert wine produced in the health and climatic micro-region of Solnechnaia Dolina (Sun Valley"). An intense ruby red, it has a soft, generous flavor.

Шемах (*shemakh*): Azerbaidjan. Quality red table wine with a heavy body, garnet red.

Южнобережный (*yoozhnabyerizhnyi*): Crimea. The southern coast of the Crimea is famous for this type, and for other fortified wines, for which the same methods have been adopted as in the production of Port with highly gratifying results.

Ясман-Салик (*yasman saleek*): Turkmenistan. One of the most interesting dessert wines produced in the ex-Soviet states, unfortunately hard to come by on the Russian market.

SWEETS

Russian sweets and cakes are totally different from those familiar in the West. All the most famous ones are, in fact, homemade cakes without creams of any sort. For this reason we have included in the "Floury Fantasy" section many products which we would find at the bakery. Russian creams for cakes are rather a surprise to the untried palate: one part egg, two parts milk and four parts butter, is the golden rule in the making of Russian sweets. For those who like it, however, this buttery cream is a real delicacy. Whipped cream is quite unknown. Another cream that is excellent by any standards is light as a feather, made only from sugar and egg with a little milk or water, and is used for example in **птичье молоко** (*pteechi malako*) which we highly recommend you to take back to the folks at home.

Варенье (*varyenye*): special mention must be made of the exceptional Russian jam, almost exclusively homemade, but often on sale in the markets or at improvised street stalls. You needn't be wary – it is genuine and keeps well. It is made only from fruit and sugar boiled according to long-established precepts and proportions, following the traditional methods you will find under "Recipes." But most surprising is the variety of the jams: raspberry, redcurrant, gooseberry, pear, bog myrtle, quince, but also melon, wild sorb and rhubarb.

Зефир (*zifeer*): a soft, frothy sweet about the size and shape of a meringue, made of eggwhite, sugar and stewed fruit (or chopped apple).

Кекс (*keks*): similar to our sponge, compact but soft and crumbly, containing a good deal of butter. Rectangular in shape, it has a central cut right throught it. It is fairly thick and covered with icing sugar and raisins.

Корзиночка (*karzeenachka*): one of the most popular small cakes, this is a full tube of buttery cream variously flavored, and glazed.

Марципан (*martseepan*): a roll with almond paste filling.

Мороженое (*marozhinaye* – ice-cream): although many Western ice-cream bars now exist and the multinationals of the sector have invaded the market, the traditional Russian ice-cream has remained unchanged. Made only from creamy fresh milk, it comes in one flavor only, rather similar to our vanilla. It is sold ready packed in plastic cups or in cones, and it is also eaten in the winter when the ice-cream is several degrees warmer than the outside temperature! It is available in restaurants as a dessert, generally served with a chocolate sauce or with jam.

Пастила (*pastila*): fruit jelly baked in the oven. It is made with apples or summer berries and is long in shape and extremely sweet.

Пирожное (*pirozhnaye*): the general name for cakes big and small which differ from what we know as pastries in their lack of custards and creams, and for their variety of cake mixtures.

Пирожное миндальное (*pirozhnaye mindal'naye*): small almond cake, made of dark, flaky almond pastry, flat and wide, glazed but not crunchy.

Повидло (*paveedla*): a sort of fruit jelly made of fruit of second-choice quality, boiled for a short time and sieved to produce a thick, homogeneous purée. Unlike real jam (**варенье**, *varyenye*, see above) it is produced industrially and is widely used for cake fillings and sweets.

Полено (*pah-lee-no*): a chocolate roll with butter cream.

Птичье молоко (*pteechi malako*): the fantastic name (something like "birds' milk") leads one to expect something strange and delicious, and there is no disappointment when one comes to taste it. It is a soft soufflé made of egg, milk and sugar with two thin layers of sponge cake, one at the bottom and one in the middle, the whole covered with chocolate icing. The shape is rectangular, but the size varies although it is never very thick.

Сгущённое молоко (*sgooshonaye malako* – condensed milk): this is nothing more than condensed milk, but it deserves mention not only as as a specimen of industrial archeology but also because it is most decidedly delicious. It has always been sold in blue-and-white tins and goes with a number of sweets as well as being used to prepare excellent white coffee.

Торт "Прага" (*tort praga* – Prague cake): one of the best-loved cakes. A soft chocolate cake with a butter, cocoa and condensed-milk filling, covered with a thin layer of fruit purée with a chocolate glaze.

Торт слоёный (*tort slayonyi* – pastry cake): cream or jam between several pastry layers. For those who like "not-too-sweet" sweets.

Халва (*khalva*): brazil nut or almond paste mixed with caramel and shaped into long bricks, dark brown and solid. Sold by the kilo.

Эклер (*eklier*): éclairs filled with variously flavored creams.

Квас (*kvas*): drink made from fermented cereals especially rye, a slightly frothy yellow, not dissimilar to non-alcoholic beers. The flavor is, however, stronger with mint aroma and the taste of the cereals is evident. It is drunk almost exclusively in summer, well chilled, drawn from small barrels on road trolleys or in 33 cl. bottles.

Кефир (*kifeer*): of Caucasian origin, but now completely absorbed into Russian food traditions, this is a rather thin yoghurt made from special milk enzymes which produce an acid taste as well as causing alcoholic, fermentation. The freshly made product contains only 0.2/0.6% of alcohol but it is enough to give it a very particular flavor, generally much to the taste of foreigners.

Морс (*mors*): a handful of summer fruits (raspberries, blackberries, etc.) is put to boil in a liter of water; the result is a mild-tasting drink, extremely pleasant, neither too sweet nor too diluted, perfect to have with a meal (especially seeing that Russian mineral waters are often not much liked by foreigners owing to their over-rich mineral content). It is served chilled, in large flasks and it is most frequently prepared with bog myrtle, rare in many countries, but very flavorsome (**Клюквенный морс**, *klyookvinyi mors*).

Нарзан (*narzan*): a mineral water bottled in Georgia and famous since the times of the Czars. It is easily the best of all mineral waters, being free of those unpleasant twangs which make the others taste more like medicine than mineral water. Apart from imported products, some fairly good Russian oligomineral waters, non-fizzy, have recently appeared on the market.

Сбитень (*sbitin*): an intensely aromatic drink made with water and honey and served hot.

Солёные грибы (*salyonyi gribee* – pickled mushrooms): a great delicacy, mushrooms are gathered all over Russia and are pickled using the juices from the mushrooms themselves (agarics, milk caps). They are also packed in jars and pressed down, or else boiled (boletus) in salted water with bay leaves and currant leaves and cloves, pepper and dill, in which they are left for 40-45 days.

Солёные овощи (*salionyi ovashi* – pickled vegetables): the tradition of pickling vegetables for the winter is still very much alive at all levels of the population. The ingredients come from summer dacha gardens. They are well worth tasting, particularly the cucumbers, so much smaller and tastier than in most countries. Tomatoes, eggplants and bell peppers are also delicious. They can be found in the market and among the starters at restaurants.

Тархун (*tarkhoon*): a drink, the main ingredient of which is tarragon, with an unusually refreshing taste. Green in color, it comes from the Caucasus and is one of the best achievements of Soviet food internationalism. Nearly flooded out by a deluge of soft drinks, it has almost disappeared from Russia today. Should you be lucky enough to discover it, do taste.

Бульон (*boolyon*): an essential ingredient of all first courses, this is a very tasty broth made from meat, fish, mushroom or vegetable stock. Chicken consommé is often served alone. It is also commonly used in sauces.

Жаркое (*zharkoye*): this is a particular kind of casserole using very little water or broth which therefore covers only part of the meat, mainly beef, cut into medium-sized pieces and cooked very slowly in a covered pan with potatoes, onions and other vegetables. It is served with **сметана** (*smitana*, see below) and parsley, piping hot in earthenware pots.

Запеканка (*zapikanka*): a general name for a variety of dishes formed of layers of different ingredients baked in the oven. It includes potato pie, pies made of cereals or a sweet **запеканка** made of ricotta cheese. It is not always in a pastry crust, but there is often a filling of minced meat.

Каша (*kasha):* a traditional cereal dish, with a high nutritional value. It may be either sweet or savoury. The types made from millet (**пшенная**, *pshenaya*), oats (**овсяная**, *afsyanaya*) and bran (**манная**, manaya) are eaten at breakfast boiled in milk, like porridge with sugar or jam. The kinds made from buckwheat (**гречневая**, *gryechnyvaya*) and rice (**рисовая**, *reesavaya*) are cooked in broth and are a crumbly mixture of separate grains. The dish may be a complete meal by itself but it is more commonly served with a main course.

Котлеты (*katlyeti*): this is a word-trap as it refers in Russian to two things which for us are totally different: breaded cutlets (**котлеты отбивные**, *katlyeti atbivneeye*) generally pork, and the more common **котлеты рубленые** (*katlyeti* *rooblinyee*) oval meatballs of beef or pork but especially chicken, minced together with onion, stale bread and milk, then coated in breadcrumbs or flour and fried. They are then served with potatoes, peas or **каша** (*kasha*, see above). They may also be made from game, fish or potatoes.

Салат (salat): among the starters, it is the salads which take the prize for inventiveness in Russian cookery: the various combinations of ingredients are infinite, while careful attention is paid to the decorative aspect of the dishes. Recipes and names vary from one place to another, even from one restaurant to another and each restaurant unfailingly boasts its own specialty. To understand something of this mouth-watering chaos, remember that one feature of most of these salads is the mixture of ingredients with contrasting flavors, cut into small cubes and dressed with mayonnaise or **сметана** (*smitana*, see below). The vegetables, whether fresh or pickled, boiled or fried, are mixed with meats, fish, eggs, cheese. Onion, garlic and parsley are common ingredients. Salads are always served cold in a small plate or bowl, decorated with sprigs of parsley, slices of tomato, hard-boiled eggwhites in rings, radish or carrot.

Сметана (*smitana*): a rich, thick fermented cream like American sour cream. An essential dressing for soups, second courses, sauces and salads, it is also used in cakes and in some pastries. It gives that slightly acidulous taste so characteristic of Russian cookery.

Соус Белый (*sowoos byelyi* – white sauce): this is a flour-based sauce with broth; cooked with parsley, celery, onion and a bay leaf all chopped finely. It is used on boiled meats, especially white meats.

Соус Красный (*sowoos krasnyi* – red sauce): a sauce made from flour and tomato purée, thinned with broth and flavored with browned onions, carrots and parsley, pepper and a red liqueur wine. It is used on meatballs, roasts and stewed meats.

Соус-хрен (*sowoos khryen* – horseradish sauce): minced horseradish mixed with vinegar, salt and sugar forms a hot sauce used on all meats, many starters and fish.

Шашлык (*shashleek*): originally a traditional Georgian dish, it has now been assimilated into Russian cooking with a series of variations. Chunks of meat, mainly beef and pork, are grilled over charcoal and accompanied by rice and vegetables.

В сметане (*fsmetanee*): a vegetable or fish dish in which **сметана** (*smetana,* see "The Basics") plays an all-important part, particularly in those stews with a **сметана** sauce. For those who love the "Queen" of Russian cookery.

Домашний (*damashnyee*): it means "homemade" and is found quite frequently in restaurants particularly in connection with egg noodles. We recommend the Russian stuffed noodles, also the fettucine type (**пельмени**, *pil'myeni* and **лапша**, *lapsha*, see "National Dishes").

Жареный (*zharinyee*): the term indicates foods fried in butter or animal fats and roasted in the oven. From fried potatoes to beef or game, a wide selection of many foods all characterized by distinctive, forceful flavors.

Заливной (*zalivnoy* – in gelatine): boiled fish (especially perch, pike and sturgeon), beef and pork can be served as cold starters in their own broth jelly.

Запечённый (*zapichonyee*): describing mainly breaded fish baked in the oven. These are crisp, dry dishes much less fatty than fried foods.

Из (*ees*): a very frequent term neaming "of" or "made of" or "from," hence indicating the basic or characteristic ingredient of a dish.

Икра (*ikra*): not only caviar, but also boiled vegetables roughly chopped and mixed to form a kind of thick paté.

Отварной (*atvarnoy* – boiled meat): various good cuts of beef can be used. The stock is flavored with carrots, turnips, leeks, bay leaves and pepper. It is then filtered and used to make the horseradish sauce with which to serve the meat.

По- (*po* – "-style" or "à la...") generally followed by an adjective indicating nationality, such as Russian, Polish, Georgian, or else a city like the famous Kiev meatballs (**котлеты по-киевски**, *katlyeti pakeeyefski*, see "Dishes of the ex-Soviet States"). They are popular, widespread variations of a well-known dish or of an imported specialty, occasionally cleverly re-invented.

Пюре (*pyooray*): any purée of vegetables or chopped fruit, sieved or mashed, raw or boiled. The blackcurrant, strawberry and raspberry purées are excellent.

Рагу (*ragoo*): the Russian meat sauce is not like ours and is not used on pasta. It is a stew of diced meat and one or more vegetables, simmered slowly, or else an all-vegetable dish made in the some way. Generally spicy and hot.

С яблоками (*syablakami* – with apples): a cooking method for duck, goose and game birds, which indicates stuffing the cleaned bird with plenty of sliced apple. Once the bird is cooked, the apple is removed and served with the meat. It gives a decidedly sweet flavor to the dish.

Суп-пюре (*soop-pyooray*): a cream soup, generally vegetable, less dense than a purée. The vegetables are first stewed then chopped and mixed with boiling milk. The same method can be used for a rice soup or meat soup.

Тушёный (*tooshonyi* – stew): indicating stewed food in general, either baked in the oven or on the stove. Used both for meats and for vegetables.

Азу (*az<u>oo</u>*): a main course. Of Caucasian origin, it is vaguely reminiscent of Arabian and Mediterranean meat or vegetable stews although the pickled gherkins give it a most distinctive flavor. It consists of pieces of meat, generally beef, first fried with tomato purée then stewed with potatoes and pickled gherkins.

Антрекот (*antre<u>kot</u>*): a main course. An entrecote steak, not very thick, cooked in a pan and served with melted butter and its own cooking juices.

Бефстроганов (*beef <u>stro</u>ganoff*): a main course. This French-style *boeuf* named after the famous Stroganoff family is one of the best dishes in Russian restaurants. Fillet or rump steak is generally used, cut into thin strips and served in the rich tomato sauce, flour diluted in broth and **сметана** (*smit<u>a</u>na*, see "The Basics").

Биточки (*bit<u>o</u>chki*): a main course. Meatballs cooked as for **котлеты рубленые** (*katlyeti rooblinyi*, see "The Basics") but round instead of long.

Бифштекс натуральный (*beef<u>shteks</u> natu<u>ral</u>nyee* – steak): a main course. Generally fillet, about 3 cm. (1 ½ in) thick cooked in butter.

Бифштекс рубленый (*beef<u>shteks</u> <u>roo</u>blinyi*): a main course. Nothing to do with steak except (generally) for the cut of the meat. It is more like a hamburger, minced beef mixed with pieces of lard and flattened into a round disk. Cooked in a pan.

Борщ (*borsh* – beetroot soup): a first course. This best-known and best-loved of Russian soups is in actual fact from the Ukraine (see "Dishes of the ex-Soviet States"). The dark purple color comes from the beetroot, its main ingredient, cooked in meat broth together with cabbage, carrot, potato, onion and tomato; **сметана** is added just before it is served.

Ботвинья (*botveenya*): a first course. An unusual chilled soup based on **квас** (*kvas*, see "Other Specialties"), a drink made from fermented cereals in which is mixed a purée of boiled spinach and sorrel. Salt, sugar and mustard are added; before it is put on the table diced cucumber, chives and dill are also added. A second version exists, as eccentric as it is aristocratic, a great favorite in the nineteenth century but now almost never to be found: the ingredients are sturgeon, watermelon, currants and spinach.

Винегрет (*vinigryet*): a starter. Salad with a sour dressing of oil and vinegar similar to the French vinaigrette. The ingredients are potatoes, beetroots and carrots boiled and diced, fresh cucumber or gherkin and sauerkraut.

Вырезка жареная (*viriska zharinaya*): a main course. Fatless fillet browned in a pan and served with chips or boiled potatoes, peas or boiled rice.

Говядина отварная с хреном (*gavyadina atvarnaya skhryenam* – boiled beef with radish sauce). A main course. This is a chance to try one of the most typical Russian dishes of boiled meat, accompanied by turnips, leeks, or other vegetables cooked in the broth, and the essential horseradish sauce.

Грибной суп (*gribnoi soop* – mushroom soup). A first course. This simple, well-flavored soup is made from mushrooms, either fresh or dried, especially the boletus type, boiled together with fried onion and carrots and potatoes. **лапша** (*lapsha*, see below) or other types of Russian noodles are added. Served with **сметана**.

Грибы в сметане (*gribee fsmitani* – mushrooms with **сметана**): a main course. Simple but very tasty. It is prepared with any type of edible mushroom, boiled briefly then cooked in a pan with flour and **сметана**. The ideal accompaniment are potatoes, especially if they are fried together with the mushrooms.

Гуляш (*goolyash*): a main course. Yet another variation of the famous Hungarian goulash without paprika or spices but with tomato purée. It is generally made with a shoulder cut of beef, but it can also be made with pork or veal. The meat, diced fairly large, is browned then stewed in broth to which the tomato purée, flour and **сметана** are added, in which it is then served.

Гусь жареный (*goos zhyarinyi* – roast goose): a main course. The goose, roasted in the oven or on the grill, is traditionally served with sauerkraut or, better still, with apples cooked inside the goose itself.

Девичьи слёзы (*divichy slyozy* – maiden's tears): a first course. These are drops of boiling milk which are dripped onto an eggplant and cauliflower pie. Each drop slowly slides as it meets greater or lesser resistance according to the pine-nuts sprinkled here and there in the pastry. Crevices and hollows form spongy mouthfuls giving an extraordinary hard-soft-empty texture.

Жаркое из свинины с черносливом (*zharkoye ees svinini shernasleevam* – pork stew with prune sauce): a main course. This dish is prepared with the typical **жаркое** method (see "The Basics"), the stew is made with only a small quantity of liquid, in this case red wine and vinegar with water. During cooking it is flavored with juniper berry and bay leaves, and the slices of pork are served in a sauce made of prunes, boiled, chopped and mixed with sugar, breadcrumbs and cinnamon.

Желе (*zhelye*): a sweet. Jelly made from fresh fruit, fruit juices or syrups, flavored with citrus fruit peel and strong, sweet red wine.

Жульен (*zhoolyen*): a starter. Nothing similar to the French *Julienne*. No vegetables, but mushroom or meat (generally cooked ham and chicken) diced very small and cooked in a **сметана** sauce with flour, butter and onion. Served in small metal bowls like tiny ladles.

Заяц тушёный в сметане (*zayets tooshonyi fsmitani* – stewed hare with **сметана**): a second course. The hare is first marinated in vinegar then cooked slowly in the oven; it takes on a most unusual flavor once the sauce of **сметана** with flour and broth is added towards the end of the cooking. The accompaniments generally underline the sour feature of the dish: marinated apples, vegetables or fruit.

Зразы (*zrazi*): a main course. Rissoles of minced meat containing hard-boiled egg, browned onion and breadcrumbs.

Кабачки фаршированные овощами (*kabachkee farshirovanyi ovashami* – marrows stuffed with vegetables). Russian marrows lend themselves to being cut in half, emptied of their seeds and stuffed, for example with carrot, onion, boiled rice, tomato and parsley. Boiled then stewed, they are served in a **сметана**-based tomato sauce.

Караси в сметане *(karassee fsmitani* – carassi with **сметана**): a main course. One of the oldest traditional fish dishes which does full justice to the delicately sour flavor of the **сметана**. The carassi, small fish of the carp family, are fried, then flavored with plenty of **сметана**, and put in the oven.

Карп с красным вином (*karp skrasneem vinom* – carp with red wine): a main course. The carp is slowly cooked whole in a mixture of red wine, fish stock, cinnamon, cloves, sugar and lemon. A strong flavor for those who enjoy spicy cooking.

Картофельные котлеты (*kartofilnyi katlyeti* – potato croquettes): a vegetable accompaniment. Made with mashed potato, egg and breadcrumbs, frequently served with a mushroom sauce.

Кисель (*kissyel*): a dessert. A jelly-like drink made from blueberries, currants, raspberries, apples, apricots, or other fresh or dried fruits, or else from fruit syrups boiled and mixed with potato flour. It is more or less thick and is served cold, sprinkled with sugar. In a similar manner a special **кисель** is made of milk and cornflour.

Компот (*kampot*): a dessert. Stewed fruit served in a syrup of sugar and water, flavored with vanilla or citrus fruit peel, in which the fruit is cooked. Apples and pears are the favorites, but apricots, plums and summer berries are also used.

Котлеты пожарские (*katlyeti pazharski* – meatballs à la Pozharskiy): a main dish. Minced chicken and bread soaked then squeezed to remove the water, fried (without breadcrumbs), in butter then finished off in the oven. They look, and are, delicious: golden crisp outside with a slight fragrance of cinnamon.

Курица жареная в сухарях (*kooritsa zharinaya fsookhariakh* – breaded chicken, fried): a main course. The chicken is first boiled then divided into portions, covered with flour and breadcrumbs (in fact with **сухари** see "Floury Fantasies" – crumbled) and fried. It is one of the few dishes accompanied by a simple green salad.

Курица под белым соусом (*kooritsa pod byelym sowusam* – fowl in white sauce): a main course. Boiled fowl with a white sauce (see "The Basics") and a few spoonfuls of the broth. The rest of the broth is served separately with croutons.

Куропатки фаршированные (*koorapatki farshirovanyi* – stuffed partridge): a main course. Halfway through the cooking time, the partridges are stuffed with minced veal, egg yolk, bread soaked in milk then squeezed, and nutmeg. They are served well roasted in their own gravy sauce.

Лангет (*langyet*): a main course. A small fillet steak, shaped like a little tongue. Cooked in a pan, occasionally breaded.

Лапша (*lapsha*): a first course. Similar to Italian fettuccine with egg and often homemade. Served with meat, mushroom or chicken broth: very good.

Макароны (*makaroni*): a side dish. Russian macaroni is of soft-grain wheat, without any sort of dressing, cooked till very soft and served with meat and boiled vegetables.

Мясное ассорти (*myasnoye assartee* – mixed meats): a starter. It is a platter of cold sliced meats with cucumbers, tomato, green salad or parsley.

Окрошка (*akroshka*): a first course. A cold soup which uses **квас** (*kvas*, see "Other Specialties") as its basic ingredient instead of broth. Beetroot, boiled carrot and potatoes, fresh cucumber and chopped chives are added. Occasionally boiled meat or ham is used. Served cold – or better still, chilled – with a sauce of **сметана**, egg yolk, mustard, salt and sugar.

Омлет (*amlyet* – omelette): a side dish or a dessert. Russian omelette, thick and spongy, is served mainly at breakfast and has various fillings (mince, chives or other greens). The sweet omelette with jam, nuts or honey is also common.

Пельмени (*pilmyeni*): a first course. Disks of meat-filled pasta similar to Italian tortellini but larger. The filling is beef or pork with a good deal of onion, but may also be fish. The Siberian version is well known and, if homemade, they are excellent while at a restaurant they often prove disappointing. As with all Russian pasta dishes, there is no sauce – they are simply boiled and served with a little butter, **сметана**, vinegar or mustard. The version cooked in broth is therefore more to our taste.

Печёнка в сметане (*pichonka fsmitani* – liver with **сметана**): a main course. The liver – veal, goose or duck – is cut into long strips, floured, fried then finished in the pan with the addition of onions and **сметана**.

Пикули (*pikoolee*): a side dish. A mixture of finely chopped vegetables cooked in a vinegar sauce that is highly spiced. Generally tiny cucumbers, onions, beans, peas and cauliflower are used. It is both a vegetable and a sauce used with meat and fish.

Поросёнок заливной (*parasyonak zalivnoy* – pork in gelatine). A starter. A baby piglet, jointed and boiled then "put together" again in its gelatine on the serving plate, is one of the greatest delicacies as a starter.

Поросёнок фаршированный гречневой кашей (*parasyonak farshirovanyi gryechnivai kashei*: a main course. This is a dish suitable for a big gathering and is typical of country eating-places. The roast piglet is served whole, stuffed with **гречневая каша** (*gryechnivaya kasha*, see "The Basics") and fried chitterlings.

Рагу из овощей (*ragoo eez avasheyi* – vegetable sauce): a main dish. A filling, richly flavored dish which is made by partially frying potatoes then stewing them very slowly together with carrots, turnips, cabbage, beans, peas, tomatoes and onion. The mixture becomes homogeneous, almost a thick cream, and is generally served cold.

Рагу из рубца (*ragoo ees rooptdsa* – tripe ragout): a main dish. As in other countries, tripe is not widely used and is closely linked to local custom. The tripe, after cleaning, is boiled at length, first blanched in the pan then stewed with tomato sauce, fried potatoes, onion and carrot with black pepper and a bay leaf.

Рассольник (*rassolnik*): a first course. A light, thin

soup with the delicate sour flavor of gherkins; the brine from which is added to the broth (of meat or sometimes fish or mushroom). The other ingredients are potatoes and onions.

Ромштекс (*ramshteks*): a main course. A thick slice of beef breaded and fried, flavored with garlic and served in its cooking juices, and unfailingly accompanied by chips.

Ростбиф (*rostbeef*): a main course. The joint of beef is cooked rare, juicy and pink; it can be served hot in its own gravy with horseradish and boiled vegetables, or cold with mayonnaise and cucumbers and tomatoes.

Салат из квашеной капусты (*salat ees kvashinai kapoosti* – salad with sauerkraut): a starter. Sauerkraut with a dressing of oil, salt, sugar and onions. Sometimes apples or red bilberries marinated in vinegar are added.

Салат из крабов (*salat ees krabaf* – crab salad): a starter. The crab flesh is generally served together with lettuce, hard-boiled eggs and chopped parsley all mixed with mayonnaise.

Салат из креветок (*salat ees krivyetak* – crayfish salad): a starter. The crayfish flesh is mixed with boiled rice and chopped hard-boiled egg, parsley. Other herbs are added and a mayonnaise dressing completes the dish.

Салат из свежих огурцов и помидоров (*salat ees svezhick agoortsof ee pamidoraf* – fresh cucumber and tomato salad): a starter. Tomatoes and fresh cucumbers are sliced with hard-boiled egg and chives or onion. The dressing is **сметана** or mayonnaise.

Салат из свежих помидоров и маринованных огурцов (*salat ees svezhikh pamidoraf ee marinovanykh agoortsof* – tomato and gherkin salad): a starter. The tomatoes and gherkins are sliced with thin slices of onion, chopped garlic, parsley and basil, with an oil dressing.

Салат из свёклы (*salat ees svyokli* – beetroot salad): a starter. Diced beetroot and nuts, with mayonnaise.

Салат "Медный всадник" (*salat myednyi fsadnik* – "Bronze Knight's Salad"): a starter. A St. Petersburg specialty. The name comes from the statue of Peter the Great, the symbol of the city. Boiled cod fillet is chopped and mixed with diced gherkin and marinated mushrooms. Spiced with pepper and cinnamon, it is served cold with boiled potatoes, onion and radishes.

Салат оригинальный (*salat ariginalnyi* – original salad): a starter. Not a common salad, rather imaginative with its sweet-and-sour flavor. It is made in two layers: the lower one being sliced onions and chopped apple, the upper one grated cheese and thinly sliced hard-boiled eggs with mayonnaise. It is eaten without mixing the two layers.

Салат столичный (*salat stalichnyi* – salad of the Capital): a starter. It is also found under other names (i.e. **оливье**, *olivye*), this is the nearest thing to "Russian salad" as we know it. It contains not only peas, carrots, gherkins, potatoes and mayonnaise, but also boiled meat, particularly chicken, or ham, and chopped hard-boiled eggs. The different ingredients are mainly blended together by the potatoes with less mayonnaise than in the Western version. There is no gelatine, therefore the single flavors are identifiable, even from one forkful to the next.

Сарделки (*sardyelki*): a main course. A kind of beef and pork sausage finely minced, either boiled or fried and served with a tomato sauce or with an onion and vinegar sauce.

Снежки из яблок (*snizhkee ees yablak*): a dessert; stiffly whipped eggwhite mixed with apple purée, sugar syrup and biscuit crumbs.

Солянка мясная (*salyanka misnaya*): a first course. Gherkins, capers, olives and chili make this soup hot and spicy, the meat broth is rich with pieces of beef or pork in it and diced ham and wurstel. It is served with **сметана**.

Солянка рыбная (*salyanka reebnaya*): a first course. Instead of meat, this **солянка** is made from fish; the sturgeon or sterlet variety is particularly tasty.
The same word can also indicate a main course. It is a fish fillet boiled with gherkins, capers and tomato purée then baked in the oven with stewed cabbage or sauerkraut. It differs from the soup of the same name though the gherkins give a similar flavor.

Сосиски (*saseeski*): a main course. Longer and thinner than **сарделки** (*sardyelki*, see above), these are small finely minced beef and pork sausages, rather similar in texture to wurstels. They are generally fried and served with mashed potato or cabbage.

Студень (*stoodin*): a starter. A jelly-like substance made by boiling lesser quality meats (head, ears, feet), mincing them and serving cold in the broth accompanied by horseradish or mustard.

Судак заливной (*soodak zalivnoy* – luce in gelatine, see below): a main course. The gelatine covering the luce is the stock obtained boiling apart head, gills and fins of the fish itself. Served cold with horseradish sauce and mayonnaise.

Судак по-польски (*soodak papolski* – Polish luce): a main course. The luce is a freshwater fish of the same family as the perch. Boiled, filleted and divided into pieces, it is served in a sauce of butter, parsley and lemon mixed with the stock in which it was boiled.

Суп-пюре из курицы (*soop-pyoorei ees kooritsi*): a first course. An elaborate, refined dish to be ordered only when the chef of the restaurant is totally trustworthy. It is a purée of boiled, finely chopped chicken in a flour, butter and strong stock sauce. Before serving, further broth, hot milk, egg yolk and butter are added, and chopped chicken is sprinkled on top. For weight-watchers.

Сырный салат (*sirnyi salat* – cheese salad): a starter. Salad with one or more types of diced or grated cheese with chopped garlic. Mixed with mayonnaise.

Тефтели (*tiftyeli*): a main course. Meatballs fried in breadcrumbs or flour then stewed in tomato sauce in which they are served.

Утка жареная в винном соусе (*ootka zharinaya veennam sowoosi* – duck in wine sauce): a main course. A simple dish but very tasty and spicy. The roast duck is served covered in a sauce made from the cooking juices, red wine, pepper, lemon and sardines reduced to a pulp.

Уха (*ookha*): a first course. A thick fish soup, using only the liquid or the boned fish in pieces. Made with any type of fresh fish, in particular sterlet and perch, with onion, carrot, parsley and sometimes potatoes in the broth.

Фаршированная щука (*farshirovanaya shooka*) – stuffed pike): a main course. An elaborate, impressive dish prepared for special occasions. Generally ordered for two or three people. The whole skin of the perch is stripped off and stuffed with the flesh of the same fish minced with onion, garlic, bread, salt and pepper. It is then boiled, divided into portions, and then put together again on the serving dish, with a little of its broth added. It is eaten with horseradish sauce.

Фасолевый суп (*fasolivyi soop* – haricot bean soup): a first course. The beans are boiled for a long time with fried onion and carrot. Served with **сметана** and chives.

Филе (*filye* – fillet): a main course. Generally one of the best cuts served in restaurants, thick, tender and without fat.

Форшмак (*farshmak*): a hot starter. A pie with beef and mutton minced with herring and onion, potato, butter and flour.

Холодец (*khaladyets*): a starter. Similar to **студень** (see above) but generally made with pork.

Цыплята жареные (*tsiplyata zharinyi* – roast spring chicken): a main course. It is the most common name for roast chicken, not only spring chicken. The best known is without doubt **цыплёнок табака** (*tsiplyonak tabaka*), see "Dishes from the ex-Soviet States."

Шашлык из осетрины (*shashleek ees asitreeni* – grilled sturgeon on the spit): a main dish. A delicate, delicious fish dish, an ideal way to taste sturgeon. The tender white boneless flesh of the Russian sturgeon – or better still of the beluga – is lightly grilled, never dried out, quite juicy and extremely tasty. Served with a slice of lemon and grilled vegetables.

Шашлык из угря (*shashleek ees oogrya* – eel on the spit): a main course. Cooked when the charcoal embers are almost out, therefore lightly smoked, these pieces of skinned eel are all the rage at present especially in high-class restaurants. Caution is, however, advisable in Moscow or further south as eels come only from the Baltic region.

Шницель (*shnitsel*): a main dish. Pork or veal cutlet either in the pan or breaded with egg and breadcrumbs. A distant relation of wiener schnitzel.

Щи (*shee*): a first course. This is perhaps the oldest, most traditional Russian dish. Of all the vegetables cooked in meat broth, the prevalent flavor is that of cabbage accompanied by potatoes, carrots, onion, tomatoes and herbs. Occasionally flour cooked in butter is added, but the best **щи** are those in which the particular sour taste of the **сметана** is countered by that of apples and berries marinated in vinegar. There are numerous other versions of **щи** in which the basic cabbage is replaced by sauerkraut, spinach, tender nettles or sorrel.

Эскалоп (*escalop*): a main course. In Russia the cutlets are veal, pork or even mutton slices, but very large. Two generally make up a portion and they are usually cooked in the pan and served with their own juice. On the other hand, they may be made with onion, mushrooms or a tomato sauce.

Ягоды со взбитыми сливками (*yagadi sa vzbeetymi sleefkami* – summer berries with cream): a dessert. If by any chance you have any room left, this is the sweet to choose. The cream is the imported spray type, but the fruits are a delicious, generous selection. Ideal in a country restaurant.

Язык отварной (*izeek atvarnoy* – boiled tongue): a starter. Beef, veal or pork tongue, boiled and spiced, is served cold, sliced with tomatoes, cucumbers or peas.

Яичница (*eeshnitsa* – omelette): a side dish. It is one of the basics of home cookery, not so common in restaurants. The infinite variety pays tribute to the skill of simple people in creating such a tasty dish from eggs served, for example, with fried black bread and tomatoes, or else with spinach, potatoes, **сметана**, ham, lard.

DISHES FROM THE EX-SOVIET STATES

United within one frontier on the map for centuries, or even only for fifty years, the countries which have emerged from the disintegration of the Soviet Union have always been linked together by strong though contradictory cultural ties and inextricable reciprocal influences. In this most complex situation, cookery is no exception: to what local tradition do you ascribe one of those Georgian dishes which are much more popular in Russia than in Tbilisi? And how do you sort out the endless disputes in the love-hate Slav relationship between the Ukraine and Russia which are based on the "which came first, the chicken or the egg" concept? The only certainty in such an intricate web is that Russia, at the center of all exchanges, has gained immensely from the appropriation of flavors and fragrances, more or less exotic, which go to prove her eclectic vocation. Thus it becomes possible to visit Russia yet taste many of the other national dishes described below, especially if you have the chance of going to one of the many Georgian or Uzbekistan or oriental restaurants in Moscow or in Saint Petersburg.

GEORGIA

European in culture and tradition, Georgia has, however, always been a frontier land, a bridge reaching towards Asia. The Eastern influence is clearly felt in the variety and originality of its food which is the most popular of all the ex-Soviet States on an international scale.
There is a nomadic "Tartar" preference for grilled meats, often cooked together with vegetables. The latter, especially eggplant and beans, play a great part, as do walnuts and hazelnuts. An elaborate sour sauce is made with walnuts, with broth and vinegar.
There is a prevalent spicy flavor due to the frequent presence

of a sour ingredient which may be from a purée of plums (**тьемали** *t'yemali*), or tomatoes or fermented milk. Many spices and herbs are used: parsley, basil, chives, as well as dill, tarragon, savory and wild coriander.

Бастурма *(bastoorma)*: a main course. Beef stew in a tomato and sour-milk sauce. The meat has a most distinctive fragrance, as it is left to marinate for many hours in grated carrot, grated onion, garlic, pepper and lemon.

Икра из баклажанов (*ikra ees baklazhanaf* – a paté of eggplant): a starter. A hot, spiced paté of chopped vegetables, served cold and spread on bread. The eggplant is grilled, then cooked peppers and tomatoes are added with onion, vinegar, garlic and pepper.

Лобио (*lobyo)*: a starter. A very common dish of cold green beans with numerous possible variations. The boiled beans, either whole or more frequently crushed, are highly spiced and form a purée with chopped onion, vinegar, garlic and pepper.

Харчо (*kharcho*): a first course. The most typical of the soups. Thick and hot, made with pieces of fatty beef, onion, parsley, wild coriander, pepper, garlic and rice. The sour plum purée **тьемали**, *t'yemaly* is added.

Цыплёнок табака (*tsiplyonak tabaka*): a main course. One of the most common Georgian dishes in Russia, it is a young cockerel roasted in a pan, crispy brown because it is pressed flat under a weight while being cooked. Hot and peppery.

Чехохбили (*chekhokhbeeli*): a main course. A fowl cut in pieces, browned, boiled then stewed until it almost falls apart, together with onions, tomato purée and a bay leaf.

Чихиртма (*chikheertma*): a first course. Saffron and egg yolk color it to a bright yellow and give this soup with the added vinegar, a particular flavor. It is a meat broth with small pieces of beef and chopped onion.

Шашлык (*shashleek*): a main course. It is the Georgian meat dish *par excellence* using fillet steak. Unlike the "Russianized" version, the real Georgia **шашлык** is cooked whole on the spit, very slowly, over a charcoal grill and only divided into single portions when it is done. Tomatoes are then roasted on the embers to go with it; it is also accompanied by a very spicy red sauce. Other types of **шашлык** are **бастурма** (*bastoorma*, see above), highly flavored pork or mutton, and eggplant cooked on the spit together with the pieces of meat.

Uzbekistan

Rich and varied, with a decided preference for first courses and pasta dishes, Uzbekistan cuisine can be compared to Italian food. **плов** (*plof*, see below), for instance, is the basic everyday rice dish and has endless variations. The flavors are, however, exotic with a number of spices, many pickled vegetables, and the absolute predominance of mutton among meat. The main courses are less typical; **шашлык** (*shashleek*, see above) is common here, too. The sweets are very good, none of them too sweet.
But a meal doesn't end here: the tourist lucky enough to visit Samarkand or Bukara will have quite exceptional fruit – melons, watermelons, peaches, apricots – so sweet and juicy

that they beat all biological plantations hollow. All greed is justifiable – but take care – Montezuma's ambush is just around the corner.

Анор ва пиез (*anor vapeeyes*): a starter. Salad of onions and sour pomegranate. The onions are sliced very thinly then scalded in boiling water and mixed with the whole seeds and the juice of the pomegranate. The flavor is unusual and intriguing, but you have to be an onion lover.

Лагман (*lagman*): a first course. A type of pie using long, flat pasta similar to the Russian **лапша** (*lapsha*, see "National Dishes"). A rich layer of sauce prepared beforehand from mince, potatoes, carrots, turnips, beetroot, spring cabbage, tomatoes, pepper and garlic, between two layers of pasta. The same sauce is used to cover the top of the pie.

Манты (*mantee*): a first course. Even larger than **пельмены** (*pil'myeni*, see "National Dishes"). Flat disks of pasta, not more than three or four to each portion, filled with minced beef or mutton with onion, pepper, and chopped lard. Served boiled, in broth or with **сметана** (*smitana*, see "The Basics").

Плов (*plof*): a first course or complete meal. It is the basic dish of Uzbekistan cookery. At first sight it looks like rice cooked with vegetables and meat, but the dish, if the old traditions are respected, has a real ritual about it. First of all, the saucepans are very big, preferably cast-iron; then during the cooking process the rice is always the top layer and never mixes with the other ingredients: mutton, chicken or game cut into pieces, chopped carrots and onions, chili and other spices, all already slowly cooked for a long time until thick in the lard which has been slowly melted. Meat, onions and carrots are present in nearly all the variations of this basic recipe among which **плов** should be mentioned – rice boiled till soft with peas and that with fig-leaves stuffed with mutton.

Салат сузма (*salat sootsma*): a starter. A salad with radishes, cucumbers and onion all finely chopped with a **сузма** dressing, **сузма** being a typical product derived from sour milk. Many herbs are added: chives, dill and wild coriander.

Ukraine

Whether a poor relation, or the cradle of Russian culture, the Ukraine boasts a good variety of dishes which, though similar in character and ingredients to Russian cuisine, show a decided tendency for rich, full flavors and a profusion of sauces. If on the one hand Ukrainian cookery keeps up the old traditions of the countryfolk, on the other, there is a notable influence of the important culinary tradition from neighboring Poland.

Борщ (*borsh* – beetroot soup): a first course. The people are very proud of the Ukrainian origin of this most famous of soups and hold themselves to be the sole possessors of those little secrets essential to its correct preparation. Unlike the Russian version, in the Ukrainian **борщ**, vegetables are not only boiled but in part also stewed. The ingredients are more or less the same, but great care is given to the different boiling times needed for the potaotes, the cabbage, the stewed beetroot, the browned onions, carrots and parsley and the garlic. The broth is not meat broth, but is made from

грудинка (*groodeenka*, see "Preserved Meats"), fatty smoked bacon, and is rather spicy; but according to the experts the secret of the flavor lies in the pieces of lard containing garlic, onion and parsley.

Вареники (*varyeniki*): a starter or a dessert. Fairly large rounds or triangles of egg pasta stuffed and folded. They are boiled briefly to leave the pasta quite hard. As for the Russian **пирожки** (*pirashkee*, see "Floury Fantasies") **вареники** can have sweet or savory fillings, but the most famous without doubt are those with fresh wild cherries served with sugar and the juice of the cherries themselves. **вареники** with ricotta cheese are not so sweet, while among the many savoury fillings there are potato and mushroom, cabbage or meat. This is considered the Ukrainian national dish.

Галушки (*galooshki*): croquettes made from flour, butter and eggs, boiled then fried. Golden outside and thick-textured inside, they can be served by themselves with **сметана** or butter, or else as a side-dish for soups. A similar dish exists in Russia, called **клёцки** (*klyotski*).

Голубцы (*gah-loob-tsy*): a main course. Large rolls of cabbage leaves stuffed with mince and rice and stewed in a **сметана** sauce, tomato purée and flour in which they are then served. The filling can also be of vegetables (onion, turnip, carrot) with hard-boiled egg, and always with rice.

Котлеты по-киевски (*katlyeti pakeeyefskee* – Kiev meatballs): a main dish. Rolled breaded chicken breasts stuffed with minced chicken, mushrooms and melted butter which softens the flavor and gives the impression of warmth and softness when they are cut.

Ряженка (*ryazhinka*): a particular type of yoghurt made from pasteurized milk and cream mixed and boiled at a high temperature for some time.

AZERBADJAN

Azerbadjan cookery is notable in particular for mutton dishes, some of which are internationally famous. Many are specialties which have been assimilated with significant variations such as the Azerbadjan variant of **плов** (*plof,* Uzbekistan) and of **пельмени** (*pil'myeny,* see "National Dishes").

Люля кебаб (*lyoolya kebab*): a main course. Mutton sausages flavored with onion. To be grilled on skewers and served with onion and tomatoes, all grilled over charcoal.

Пити (*peeti*): a first course. A spicy soup served in a special earthernware bowl after which it is named. The broth is prepared with pieces of mutton and peas and has a very particular flavor. Potatoes, Mirabella plums or tomatoes, onion and pork fat are also added.

SPECIALTIES FROM OTHER COUNTRIES

Босбаш (*bosbash*): Abkhazia, Armenia. A lamb stew cooked with tomatoes, peppers and peas with a particular sweet-and-sour flavor derived from chopped apple.

Камбала аврора (*kambala avrora* – Aurora sole): Lithuania. Browned over a very low heat, floured filleted strips of sole are cooked in a thin layer of finely chopped carrot, onion and parsley in a sauce of **сметана** (*smitana*, see "The Basics") and tomato purée.

Мамалыга (*mamaleega*): Moldavia and Caucasian Republics. A thick paste-like substance of cornflour boiled in water then mixed with milk. It can be left to cool and used instead of bread during meals.

Окунь в молоке (*okun' vmalakye* – perch in milk): Beloruss. A simple, delicate dish with an exotic combination of flavors from the cooked vegetables and milk. The filleted perch is cut into small pieces and left to cook slowly with carrots, onions and potatoes. Milk is added at the end with butter melted into the resulting sauce.

In Georgia, Armenia and some of the Asian republics, some practical problems may arise, as independence has brought with it a strong tendency to revive local alphabets which are quite undecipherable. However, common business sense overshadows patriotic pride so that Cyrillic is still used on most menus.

With a pinch of extra effort, the unusual and intriguing flavors of Russian cookery can become part of the repertory of your own home cooking. Of course, not all ingredients or their equivalents can be found thousands of kilometers away in a totally different gastronomic culture. You may have to adapt some ingredients to your own taste and decide whether or not to revive the use of animal fats so favored by former generations in the West, but the results will be encouraging. The ever-present **сметана** (*smitana*, see "The Basics") will cause another difficulty; the complicated and imaginative solutions proposed to supply a substitute are all more or less disappointing. You will, however, obtain something which is at least satisfactory if you use two parts of kitchen cream and one of whole-milk, plain yoghurt.

All recipes are for four generous portions.

БЕФСТРОГАНОВ (Beef Stroganoff)
(*beefstroganaf*)

Ingredients:

slices of beef	*550 g*	*(1¼ lb)*
broth	*160 g*	*(5 oz)*
tomato purée	*50 g*	*(2 oz)*
cream	*100 g*	*(4 oz)*
full cream yoghurt	*50 g*	*(2 oz)*
flour	*20 g*	*(1 oz)*
onion	*100 g*	*(4 oz)*
3 spoons oil		
salt, pepper		

Preparation:
Flatten the beef slices by beating gently. They should be about 5 mm (about $^1/_3$ in) thick. Cut them into strips 3 or 4 cm (about $^3/_4$ in) long. The onions (use more if you wish) are cut into chunks and browned, then the meat is stirred in and cooked over the heat for 5-7 minutes; at this point add the tomato purée and continue cooking for another 5 minutes. Meanwhile prepare the **сметана** with two parts cream and one yoghurt, and the broth (you can use broth from a cube): pour the mixture into the pan with a handful of flour. Add salt and pepper and stir to mix the sauce in well; leave to thicken on the heat for about five minutes.

БЛИНЫ
(*blinee*)

Ingredients:

flour	*600 g*	*(1 $^1/_3$ lb)*
butter	*40 g*	*(2 oz)*
yeast	*25 g*	*(1 oz)*

2 eggs
3 glasses of milk (or water)
a spoon and a half of sugar
a spoon of salt

Preparation:
Dissolve the yeast in a glass of hot milk (or water), sprinkle in half the flour and mix until smooth. Cover with a cloth and leave to rise in a warm place. When the mixture has risen, add the melted butter, the salt, sugar and two raw eggs, work in well and mix with the remaining flour, add the two glasses of milk or water. Leave the mixture aside until it is well risen (about three hours in all are necessary for it to rise). The most

delicate moment is certainly the frying. The pan should be cast-iron or at least very heavy. The oil must be very hot; spoon in the mixture so it forms circular portions 3-4 mm (or about ¼ in) in thickness – it should start to bubble and the fritter will be crisp and golden. If there is too much smoke, lower the heat. When the underside of the fritter starts to go golden brown, turn it using a knife to let the other side cook. As soon as they are ready (and if you are making many, you should use more than one pan) they should be served – smoking hot – with jam or chestnut cream or nutella cream; but don't forget that **блины** go perfectly well with savoury foods; if caviar isn't served, use smoked salmon, anchovies or shrimps.

БОРЩ (Beetroot soup)
(borsh)

Ingredients:

stew meat (beef or veal)	*500 g*	*(1 lb)*
beetroot	*300 g*	*(11 oz)*
cabbage	*300 g*	*(11 oz)*
carrots	*150 g*	*(5 oz)*
onions	*100 g*	*(4 oz)*
tomato purée	*100 g*	*(4 oz)*
1 spoon vinegar		
1 spoon sugar		
salt, pepper, a bay leaf		

Preparation:
First of all prepare a good beef broth. Roughly slice the beetroot, carrots, and onions and put them into a saucepan. Add a cup of the broth, the sugar and the tomato purée,

cover the saucepan and bring to a boil on a high heat. Turn down the heat and continue to cook for 30 minutes, mixing occasionally and adding further broth if necessary. Now add the cabbage, thinly sliced and continue cooking for a further 15 minutes. Remove the fat from the surface of the broth and pour it into the saucepan, adding salt, pepper, vinegar and the bay leaf. Cook for a further 10 minutes, then serve with a piece of the boiled meat to each portion. If you like **сметана** (or the substitute we have suggested in the introduction to this section), you can use it to flavor the *borsh* in each plate.

БОРЩ УКРАИНСКИЙ (Ukranian beetroot soup)
(borsh ookraeenskee)

Ingredients:

pork (for boiling) or	*500 g*	*(1 lb)*
smoked bacon	*300 g*	*(11 oz)*
beetroot	*400 g*	*(14 oz)*
potatoes	*400 g*	*(14 oz)*
cabbage	*300 g*	*(11 oz)*
ripe tomatoes	*100 g*	*(4 oz)*
carrots	*70 g*	*(3 oz)*
onions	*30 g*	*(1 oz)*
tomato purée	*50 g*	*(2 oz)*

2 cloves garlic
½ spoon sugar
1 spoon vinegar
salt, pepper, dill, a bay leaf

Preparation:
Did you like the **борщ**? Did you try the recipe above as

soon as you got the chance? Now how about comparing the Ukrainian **борщ**, which takes a bit longer than the Russian version, but certainly provides a more intense, original flavor. In the first place, the broth is made from pork or from a piece of smoked bacon to give an even more distinctive flavor, and it should be boiled for no less than two hours. Thirty minutes before the end of that time, add the peeled potatoes cut into cubes. At 25 before, in goes the thinly sliced cabbage; at 15, add the onions and carrots, lightly fried with some parsley; at 12 it's the turn of the beetroot, parboiled beforehand in half a cup of the broth, the tomato purée and the vinegar. At 8 minutes before, the fresh tomatoes, roughly cut. Add salt, pepper and a bay leaf at 5 minutes before the end of cooking time. Just two minutes before the end of the cooking time add the crushed garlic and at the same time the pieces of lard (absolutely necessary) into which you have rubbed garlic, onion and parsley. The **борщ** is left to cool for a quarter of an hour, and then it is served with the boiled pork and the **сметана** sauce (two parts of yoghurt to one part of cream) to taste.

ВАРЕНЬЕ ИЗ ЯБЛОК (Apple jam)
(varyenye ees yablak)

Ingredients:

apples	*1 kg*	*(2 lb)*
sugar	*1.3 kg*	*(2½ lb)*
water	*80 cl*	*(1½ pt)*

Preparation:
Without claiming to have made a wonderful discovery, here is the Russian recipe for jam for comparison with other

traditions – with perhaps even some forgotten tips also used by our own grandmothers.
First of all, prepare the syrup, boiling all the water with the sugar and stirring until the latter is completely dissolved. As soon as the water returns to a boil, remove the syrup from the heat and filter. In the meantime, peel, core and slice the apples, parboil in boiling water for 4 minutes after which plunge them immediately into cold water so they do not go brown.
Pour half the syrup you have made onto the apples just to cover them, and leave them aside for three hours. Bring the apples and syrup to a boil, removing the froth as it forms, and let them boil for 5-7 minutes. It is very important to judge the correct instant in which to interrupt the cooking – when the froth starts to gather only in the middle of the saucepan, or when a drop of syrup, dripped onto a plate, doesn't run off. If in doubt, remove from the heat after 6 minutes. Leave the jam aside for 6-8 hours or all night, covered with foil, then repeat the boiling operation 3 or 4 times, at the same intervals of time.

ГРИБЫ В СМЕТАНЕ (Mushrooms with **сметана**)
(gribee fsmitani)

Ingredients:

mushrooms	*1 kg*	*(2 lb)*
potatoes	*350 g*	*(12 oz)*
cream	*140 g*	*(5 oz)*
whole cream yoghurt	*70 g*	*(3 oz)*
butter	*60 g*	*(2 oz)*
flour	*30 g*	*(1 oz)*
salt		

Preparation:
Cultivated mushrooms are perfectly adequate for this recipe if others are not available. Cleaned and rinsed, they are boiled in slightly salted water for 5-6 minutes. Drain, slice and fry for 25-30 minutes together with potatoes cut matchstick-style. When they are nearly cooked, add the flour, a little salt and mix before adding the **сметана** you have prepared with cream and whole yoghurt. Mix again well, increase the heat and cook for a further three minutes.

ЖАРКОЕ (Beef stew)
(*zharkoe*)

Ingredients:

beef (fillet or sirloin)	*600 g*	*(1 1/3 lb)*
potatoes	*400 g*	*(14 oz)*
onions	*80 g*	*(3 oz)*
broth	*200 g*	*(7 oz)*
half glass white wine		
salt, pepper, a bay leaf		

Preparation:
Cut the meat into fairly small pieces and brown them. In another pan, brown the diced potatoes and the chopped onion for a longer time. Put everything into one saucepan with the broth and stew for 30 minutes, mixing occasionally and adding further broth if necessary. Ten minutes before the meat is ready, add the white wine, salt, pepper and the bay leaf. Serve with **сметана**, prepared with two parts of cream and one of whole-milk yoghurt.

ИКРА ИЗ БАКЛАЖАНОВ (Eggplant paté)
(eekra ees baklazhanaf)

Ingredients:

eggplants	*800 g*	*(1 3/4 lb)*
fresh tomatoes	*200 g*	*(7 oz)*
peppers	*200 g*	*(7 oz)*
two onions		
garlic, vinegar, salt, pepper		

Preparation:
A cooling summer dish from Georgia, ideal for a snack or at a barbecue. Wash the eggplants, cut them in half and cook in the oven until they are soft and the skin is dark brown. Remove from the oven, peel and chop them as finely as possible, or use an electric mixer to get a mixture without lumps but not of a creamy consistency. Add salt and pepper and mix with the other ingredients which you have in the meantime prepared as follows: tomatoes and bell peppers cooked in a pan and then finely chopped together; the onion, first simply sliced and salted, left for an hour then squeezed and chopped. The paté should be as homogeneous as possible, and certainly not dry: if there is too much liquid it can be condensed over a very low heat. When cold, the paté is eaten spread on bread or toast. It can be kept for several days in the fridge.

КУЛЕБЯКА
(*koolibyaka*)

Ingredients:

flour	*400 g*	*(14 oz)*
milk	*90 g*	*(4 oz)*
yeast	*20 g*	*(1 oz)*
butter	*50 g*	*(2 oz)*
mince	*250 g*	*(9 oz)*
rice	*150 g*	*(5 oz)*

2 egg yolks and 2 hard-boiled eggs
1 dessert spoon sugar
half a dessert spoon salt

Preparation:

We have chosen one of the most famous recipes for **кулебяка**, that with mince, rice and hard-boiled eggs, but it is a dish invented on purpose to stimulate the imagination as regards the filling. There should be three fillings, if possible; one will do as long as the correct proportions are maintained between the weight of the pasta and that of the filling: more or less, one to one. The secret of **кулебяка** lies in the abundance of the fillings, intentionally over-generous – there can't be too much.

First of all, prepare a normal bread dough by dissolving the yeast in the warm milk with half the flour and half the sugar; leave it to rise then work in the two eggs, the butter, the rest of the sugar and the flour with the salt. Again leave the dough to rise, then when it gives the first sign of deflating, roll it out into a one-centimeter (or $^3/_8$ in.) thick length. Spread the first layer of filling, in this case the boiled rice (very slightly undercooked); this should be the layer with the lowest liquid content (therefore not a meat or fish filling) otherwise the lower layer of the dough will become soggy.

Then add a layer of chopped, hard-boiled egg and another of the minced meat just scalded in salted water and well drained.
Raise the long sides of the dough and join them together so that the **кулебяка** is closed into a pastry shape, place on a well-greased oven tray with the seam on the bottom. Leave it for a few minutes, then brush with egg yolk, pierce with a fork two or three times so the steam can escape, place in the pre-heated oven and bake for 35-40 minutes at medium temperature.

ПЛОВ
(*plof*)

Ingredients:

long-grain rice	*600 g*	*(1 1/3 lb)*
beef	*300 g*	*(11 oz)*
carrots	*250 g*	*(9 oz)*
onions	*25 g*	*(1 oz)*
oil and lard,		
salt, chili, caraway		

Preparation:
In Uzbekistan there are dozens of different variations of **плов**, as it is a basic dish comparable to pasta in Italy or rice in China. It is based on the Turkish recipe for *pilaf* or *pilaw*, which is now well known internationally but which is not the quick dish it is often presumed to be. The correct method takes time and care, not to mention a good portion of age-old skill in the art of cookery; this last can be only partially supplemented with the following instructions for the most common Uzbekistan **плов**.

Cut the meat into mouthful-sized cubes and fry lightly in hot oil or, better still, in accordance with the old traditions, in lard. When a crispy brown surface has formed add the carrots and onions cut into thin strips and continue frying for a few minutes.
Now transfer everything into a big saucepan and pour a liter (or about 2 pints) of boiling water onto it, add salt, chili and the spices, if you can obtain them. As soon as the liquid boils again, add the long-grain rice which should form a compact layer on top without mixing with the meat. When the rice has absorbed all the water, dig out two deep holes and pour into each, one or two spoons of boiling water. Continue cooking on a very low heat for a further 20-25 minutes, with the saucepan covered. The helpings should each contain equal portions of meat, rice and carrots – and will be generous in quantity.

РАГУ ИЗ ОВОЩЕЙ (Vegetable ragout)

(*ragoo eez avashai*)

Ingredients:

potatoes	*500 g*	*(1 lb)*
cabbage (or cauliflower)	*250 g*	*(9 oz)*
peas	*100 g*	*(4 oz)*
broth	*50 g*	*(2 oz)*
ripe tomatoes	*70 g*	*(3 oz)*
flour	*20 g*	*(1 oz)*

3 carrots
2 onions
2 turnips
3 spoons oil
salt, pepper, a bay leaf

Preparation:
The ingredients can vary according to the seasons, to tastes and also to what there is in the fridge: this is a very simple dish, tasty and wonderful on cold winter evenings. Start with the potatoes which are cut into wedges and lightly fried; then the onions, carrots and turnips, also cut into wedges, also lightly fried in the pan; the cabbage is boiled while the tinned peas are ready as they are, or else frozen peas are done together with the onions and carrots. Put all the ingredients together into a saucepan and, in a separate pan, fry the flour lightly in a little oil, add some broth (the water in which the cabbage was cooked is excellent) and the chopped tomatoes. This is then added to the saucepan, mixed with the vegetables and flavored with salt, pepper and the bay leaf; the whole is then left to stew very slowly for 15 or 20 minutes, with the potatoes requiring particular attention, so as not to overcook.

САЛАТ СТОЛИЧНЫЙ (Salad of the Capital)
(*salat staleechnyi*)

Ingredients:

potatoes	*400 g*	*(14 oz)*
gherkins	*200 g*	*(7 oz)*
peas	*150 g*	*(5 oz)*
carrots	*150 g*	*(5 oz)*
cooked ham	*100 g*	*(4 oz)*
3 eggs		
6 spoons mayonnaise		

Preparation:
The absolute minimum legacy of a gastronomic trip through Russia must without fail be your recipe for Russian salad

unmistakably different from the Russian salad your friends at home prepare. It is the details that make all the difference.

Your Russian salad must be left in the fridge on the lower shelf for at least two hours; and all the ingredients must be equally cold when it is made. The cooked ham, the peas and gherkins, if taken out of the fridge, have to reach room temperature before they touch the other boiled items which are cooling down. So start by dicing the cooked ham, bought in one single thick slice, and place it in the salad bowl.

Add the tinned peas immediately (frozen peas would require cooking in oil first, which would add an undesiderable taste). Slice the gherkins finely – the ones in brine have a more delicate flavor; homemade preserves are perhaps too much to ask, but do avoid other kinds of pickles which are commonly used. In the meantime, the other ingredients should have been boiled (beforehand if possible, but there is never time enough...) so you can shell the hard-boiled eggs and cut them up small. Scrape the carrots and dice them. The potatoes should be boiled until they crumble at the touch of the knife. Crush them until they are almost a purée, put them in the salad bowl and mix well so the ingredients are thoroughly blended. Then there is only the mayonnaise – six spoonfuls, never more than a hundred-gram (or 4 oz) jar – which you will mix in to obtain the final texture desired, with a little salt. The original recipe requires boiled chicken breast, but cooked ham is much more practical and preserves the necessary meaty taste – not too strong. However, if you have time, try the boiled chicken and you will see how the secret of the dish lies in the perfect blend and the rather colorless look of all the ingredients which, however, sustain and enhance each other's flavor.

ЩИ (Cabbage soup)
(*shee*)

Ingredients:

boiled meat (beef)	*500 g*	*(1 lb)*
cabbage	*500 g*	*(1 lb)*
potatoes	*200 g*	*(7 oz)*
fresh tomatoes	*200 g*	*(7 oz)*

2 onions
2 carrots
1 bay leaf, 1 piece of celery, parsley
salt, pepper

Preparation:
Make the meat broth, as transparent as consommé, adding a carrot, the celery and one fried onion after one hour's boiling. Continue cooking for another 45 minutes, then take out the meat and carefully filter the broth into another saucepan in which you have already put the cabbage, thickly sliced (about twenty pieces), together with the other onion and carrot sliced and lightly fried. The cabbage should cook for a total of about 30-35 minutes. The potatoes – ideally small ones, peeled and cut into 2-4 parts – are added after about ten minutes. Add the salt and pepper five minutes before the end of the cooking time together with the tomato cut into small pieces and bay leaf. The meat is generally eaten separately, but a piece can be served in each portion of soup.

ЯИЧНИЦА С ЧЕРНЫМ ХЛЕБОМ (Omelette with brown bread) (*eeshnitsa shornim khlyebam*)

Ingredients:

black bread	*130 g*	*(5 oz)*
ripe tomatoes	*100 g*	*(4 oz)*
4 eggs		
2 spoons oil		
salt, chili		

Preparation:

In conclusion we recommend this very simple recipe which you are unlikely to find in any restaurant, but which is more than likely to earn a permanent place on the home menu. It is a straightforward omelette, but transformed and exalted by the black bread.

First, obtain the bread, if possible rye bread but otherwise with mixed cereals – the German type is excellent. Ordinary brown bread will not do. Use a large frying-pan, cut the bread into small cubes and brown crisp in the oil. Add the tomatoes, thinly sliced, and let them fry together with the bread for half a minute or so. Break the eggs and spread them uniformly and cook without stirring, as for a normal omelette, adding salt and chili.

ALPHABET

Should you need to spell a word, here is the pronunciation of each of the letters of the Russian alphabet, followed by an example to help you (i.e.: *a kak akrabat* = a as in akrabat).

а	**акробат**	**й**	**йод**	**у**	**утюг**
a	*akrabat*	*i*	*yot*	*u*	*utyook*
б	**бифштекс**	**к**	**кабан**	**ф**	**фаворит**
be	*bifshteks*	*ka*	*kaban*	*ef*	*favarit*
в	**валет**	**л**	**лик**	**х**	**хобот**
ve	*valyet*	*el*	*lik*	*kha*	*khobat*
г	**газон**	**м**	**монтёр**	**ц**	**центр**
ge	*gazon*	*em*	*mantyor*	*tse*	*tsentr*
д	**декабрист**	**н**	**новатор**	**ч**	**часовня**
de	*dikabrist*	*en*	*navatar*	*che*	*chasovnya*
е	**егерь**	**о**	**облака**	**ш**	**шатун**
ye	*yegir'*	*o*	*oblaka*	*sha*	*shatoon*
ё	**ёж**	**п**	**пряник**	**щ**	**щипок**
yo	*yosh*	*pe*	*pryanik*	*sha*	*shipok*
ж	**журналист**	**р**	**робот**	**э**	**экипаж**
zhe	*zhurnalist*	*re*	*robat*	*e*	*ekipash*
з	**золото**	**с**	**солома**	**ю**	**юла**
ze	*zolata*	*es*	*saloma*	*yoo*	*yoola*
и	**индус**	**т**	**тарантас**	**я**	**якут**
ee	*eendoos*	*te*	*tarantas*	*ya*	*yakut*

The **ы**, causes a bit more trouble; it is never the first letter in a word, so you could say "**вторая буква в слове 'бык**" *(ftaraya bookva vslovi "byk"* – the second letter in "bull"). The two signs used to modify the sound of the preceding letter will have to be indicated with their Russian names: **ь = мягкий знак** *(myakhkeei znak* – weak sign) and **ъ = твёрдый знак** *(tvyordyi znak* – strong sign).

Things to remember

The shop you are looking for is **Кондитерская** *(kandeetirskaya), but cakes are frequently sold on improvised street stalls as well, in cardboard boxes tied up with string. Be especially careful of western-style cakes and sweets: because of their exorbitant prices, they may well have been on sale for a few days already, awaiting one of the nouveaux riches to come along.*

What are these / those?	**Что это такое?** *Shto eta takoye?*
What's in this cake?	**С чем этот торт?** *S chem etat tort?*
I would like an assortment of cakes	**Я бы хотел(а) несколько пирожных** *Ya bee khatyel(a) nyeskal'ka pirozhneekh*
I'd like a chocolate ice-cream with whipped cream	**Я бы хотел(а) шоколадное мороженоесо сливками** *Ya bee khatyel(a) shakaladnaye marozhnaye sasleefkami*
I'd like an ice-cream in a cup	**Я бы хотел(а) мороженое в стаканчике** *Ya bee khatyel(a) marozhnaye fstakanchiki*
Is there any chocolate in those small cakes?	**В этих пирожных есть шоколад?** *Vetikh pirozhneekh yest' shakalat?*

I have a small child / two children	**У меня маленький ребёнок/ двое детей** *Oo minya malin'kyi ribyonak / dvoy dityei*
Do you have a discount for children?	**У вас есть скидки для детей?** *Oo vas yest' skeetki dlya dityei?*
Do you have a small bed for the child?	**У вас есть детская кроватка?** *Oo va yest' dyetskaya kravatka?*
Do you have a child's menu?	**У вас есть меню для детей?** *Oo vas yest' minyoo dlya dityei?*
Can you warm the baby's bottle?	**Вы можете мне разогреть бутылочку для ребёнка?** *Vee mozhiti mnye razagryet' booteelachkoo dlya ribyonka?*
Where can I feed / change the baby?	**Где я могу покормить/переодеть ребёнка?** *Gdye ya magoo pakarmit' / piryadyet' ribyonka?*
Do you have a high chair?	**У вас есть детский стульчик?** *Oo vas yest' dyetsiy stul'chik?*
Is there a garden where the children can play?	**Здесь есть сад, где могут играть дети?** *Zdyes' yest' sat gdye mogoot igrat' dyeti?*
Please bring me a glass of water at room temperature	**Принесите мне, пожалуйста, стакан воды комнатной температуры** *Priniseeti mnye pazhalsta stakan vadee komnatnoy timpiratoori*

This does'nt work	**Это не работает** *Eta nye rabotait*
It's broken	**Это сломано** *Eta slomana*
We are still waiting to be served	**Нас всё ещё не обслужили** *Nas fsyo isho nyapsloozheeli*
The coffee is cold	**Кофе холодный** *Kofi khalodnyi*
This meat is tough	**Это мясо жёсткое** *Eta myasa zhostkaya*
The tablecloth is dirty	**Скатерть грязная** *Skatyert' griaznaya*
The room is noisy	**Эта комната шумная** *Eta komnata shoomnaya*
It's too smokey in here	**Здесь слишком накурено** *Zdyes' sleeshkam nakoorina*

Do you speak English / Italian / French?	**Вы говорите по-английски/по-итальянски/по-французски?** *Vee gavareeti paangleeski / paiital'yanski / pafrantsooski?*
I don't speak Russian	**Я не говорю по-русски** *Ya nigavaryoo paroosky*
What is your name? (formal)	**Как вас зовут?** *Kak vas zavoot?*
What is your name? (informal)	**Как тебя зовут?** *Kak tibya zavoot?*
My name is …	**Меня зовут…** *Minya zavoot …*
Do you mind if I sit here?	**Вы не возражаете, если я сяду здесь?** *Vee nivazrazhaiti yesli ya syadoo zdyes'?*
Is this place free?	**Это место свободно?** *Eta myesta svabodna?*
Where are you from?	**Откуда вы?** *Atkooda vee?*
I am from …	**Я из…** *Ya iss …*
I'm British / American	**Я днглиуднин/дмерикдмен** *Ya angleeteneeeneem / am-ayreeka reeaytz*
Can I offer you a coffee / something to drink?	**Я могу предложить вам кофе/что-нибудь выпить?** *Ya magoo pridlazhit'vam kofi / shtoniboot' veepit'?*
Yes, please / No, thank you	**Да, спасибо/нет, спасибо** *Da spaseeba / nyet spaseeba*

The first of March	**Первое марта**	*Pyervaye marta*
The second of June	**Второе июня**	*Ftaroye yoonya*
Nineteen ninety-seven	**Тысяча девятьсот девяносто сеуъмой год**	*Teesicha divyat'sot divyanosta seedmayee got*
Monday	**понедельник**	*panidyel'nik*
Tuesday	**вторник**	*ftornik*
Wednesday	**среда**	*srida*
Thursday	**четверг**	*chitvyerk*
Friday	**пятница**	*pyatnitsa*
Saturday	**суббота**	*soobota*
Sunday	**воскресенье**	*vaskrisyenye*
January	**январь**	*yanvar'*
February	**февраль**	*fivral'*
March	**март**	*mart*
April	**апрель**	*apryel'*
May	**май**	*mahhi*
June	**июнь**	*yoon*
July	**июль**	*yool*
August	**август**	*afgoost*
September	**сеньтябрь**	*sintyabr'*
October	**октябрь**	*aktyabr'*
November	**ноябрь**	*nayabr'*
December	**декабрь**	*dikabr'*

Excuse me, where is the station?	**Извините, где вокзал?** *Izvineeti gdye vagzal?*
How do I get to the airport?	**Как мне доехать до аэропорта?** *Kak mnye dayekhat' da aeraporta?*
Can you tell me the way to the station?	**Вы можете указать мне дорогу к вокзалу?** *Vee mozhiti ukazat' mnye darogoo kvagzaloo?*
Is this the way to the cathedral?	**Эта дорога ведёт в собор?** *Eta daroga vidyot fsabor?*
I am looking for the Tourist Information Office	**Я ищу бюро информации для туристов** *Ya ishyoo byooro informatsii dlya tureestaf?*
Which way must I go for …?	**По какой дороге можно добраться в …?** *Pa kakoi darogi mozhna dabratsa v …?*
How long does it take to get there?	**За сколько можно туда добраться?** *Za skol'ka mozhna tooda dabratsa?*
Excuse me, can you tell me where the … Restaurant is?	**Извините вы не знаете, где ресторан …?** *Izvineeti vee niznaiti gdye ristaran …?*

Things to remember

Western-style cafés where you can have a bite to eat and something to drink are few and far between, and expensive. In the downtown area of Moscow, however, there are a number of places where you can get an expresso coffee in fairly comfortable surroundings for about five dollars. Apart from the sign **Бар** *(bar) you can also look out for* **Кафетерий** *(kafitereei) or* **Пуб** *(poop). The* **Бистро** *(bistro) offer a wider choice on the menu while the* **Кафе** *(kafe) are at present going through a period of transformation, though by tradition they are, in fact, proper restaurants though unpretentious and cheaper.*

A black coffee / a white coffee	**Кофе/кофе с молоком** *kofi / kofi s malakom*
A glass of ale / porter please	**Среднюю кружку светлого/ тёмного пива, пожалуйста** *Sryednyuyu krooshoo svyetlava / tyomnava peeva pazhalsta*
Two cups of tea with lemon / with milk, please	**Две чашки чая с лимоном, /с мопоком пожалуйста** *Dvye chashkee chyaya slemonam / s malakom, pazhalsta*
A glass of mineral water, please	**Стакан минеральной воды, пожалуйста** *Stakan miniral'noy vadi pazhalsta*
With ice, please	**Со льдом, пожалуйста** *Sal'dom pazhalsta*
Bring me my bill, please	**Принесите счёт, пожалуйста** *Priniseety shot pazhalsta*

Good evening, we would like a table for two	**Добрый вечер, мы бы хотели столик на двоих**	*Dobryi vyechir mee bee khatyeli stolik na dvaeekh*
We'd like a table in a quiet corner	**Мы бы хотели столик в спокойном уголке**	*Mee bee khatyeli stolik v spakoinam ugalkye*
We have reserved a table for two, in the name …	**Мы заказывали столик на двоих на имя …**	*Mee zakazeevali stolik na dvaeekh na eemya…*
Is it possible to eat outside?	**Можно пообедать на воздухе?**	*Mozhna paabyedat' na vozdookhi?*
We would like a table away from / near the window	**Мы бы хотели столик далеко от окна/близко к окну**	*Mee bee khatyeli stolik daliko at akna / bliska k aknoo*
Is there an entrance for the disabled?	**Здесь есть вход для инвалидов?**	*Zdyes' yest' fkhod dlya invaleedaf?*
Do you speak English?	**Вы говорите по по-английски?**	*Vee gavareeti paangleeski?*
May we see the menu?	**Можно посмотреть меню?**	*Mozhna pasmatryet' minyoo?*
Do you have a vegetarian menu?	**У вас есть вегетарианское меню?**	*Oo vas yest' vigitarianskaye minyoo?*

What is your house specialty?	**Какое ваше фирменное блюдо?** *Kakoye vashe feermenaye blyooda?*
What do you suggest?	**Что вы нам советуете?** *Shto vee nam savyetooiti?*
What's in this dish?	**Из чего состоит это блюдо?** *Ees chivo sastaeet eta blyooda?*
Is it hot?	**Это острое?** *Eta ostraye?*
I'm allergic to chili	**У меня аллергия на перец** *Oo minya alyergeea na pyerits*
Does this dish contain any garlic / pepper?	**В этом блюде есть чеснок/перец?** *Vetam blyoodi yest' chisnok / pyerits?*
Do you have …?	**У вас есть …?** *Oo vas yest … ?*
I would like / We would like …	**Я бы хотел(а)/мы бы хотели …** *Ya bee khatyel(a) / mee bee khatyeli …*
Bring me / us …	**Приинесите мне/нам …** *Priniseeti mnye / nam …*
I would like a portion / half a portion of …	**Я бы хотел(а) порцию/половину порции …** *Ya bee khatyel(a) portsyoo / palaveenoo portsii …*
I would like to taste …	**Я бы хотел(а) попробовать …** *Ya bee khatyel(a) paprobavat' …*

Bring us some more bread, please	**Принесите, пожалуйста, ещё хлеба** *Priniseeti pazhalsta isho khlyeba*
What dishes are typical of this area?	**Какие блюда типичны для этой области?** *Kakye blyooda tipeechni dlya etai oblasti?*
What sweets / fruit do you have?	**Что у вас есть из сладкого/ из фруктов?** *Shto oo vas iest' ees sladkava / ees fruktaf?*
We would like a portion of ... with two plates	**Мы бы хотели порцию ... с двумя тарелками** *Mee bee khatyeli portsiu ... s dvumya taryelkami*
Can you bring me the salt / the pepper?	**Принесите, пожалуйста, соль/перец** *Prineseeti pazhalsta sol' / pierits*
Four coffees, please	**Четыре кофе, пожалуйста** *Chiteeri kofi pazhalsta*
Can we see the wine list?	**Можно посмотреть карту вин?** *Mozhna pasmatryet' kartu vin?*
We would like an aperitif	**Мы бы хотели аперитив** *Mee bee khatyeli apiritif*
What wine do you suggest with this dish?	**Какое вино вы советуете к этому блюду?** *Kakoye vino vee savyetuiti ketamoo blyoodu?*

Do you have you any draught beer?	**У вас есть пиво в разлив?** *Oo vas yest' peeva vrazleef?*
A bottle / A half-bottle of … please	**Бутылку/пол-бутылки …, пожалуйста** *Booteelkoo / polbooteelki … pazhalsta*
A bottle of still / sparkling mineral water, please	**Бутылку минеральной натуральной/газированной воды, пожалуйста** *Booteelkoo miniral'noi natooral'noi / gazirovanai vadee pazhalsta*
We would like some water at room temperature / chilled water	**Мы бы хотели воду комнатной температуры/из холодильника** *Mee bee khatyeli vodoo komnatnai timpiratoori / ees khaladeel'nika*
Please bring us another bottle of vodka / of wine	**Принесите, пожалуйста, ещё одну бутылку водки/вина** *Priniseeti pazhalsta isho adnoo booteelkoo votki / vina*
What wines / liqueurs are typical of this region?	**Какие вина/ликёры типичны для этой зоны?** *Kakeeye veena / likyori tipeechni dlya etai zoni?*
What liqueurs do you have?	**Какие у вас есть ликёры?** *Kakeeye oo vas yest' likyori?*
This wine has not been cooled	**Это вино не охлаждено** *Eta vino nye akhlazhdino*

Excuse me, where's the restroom?	**Извините, где туалет?** *Izvineeti gdye tualyet?*
Is there a telephone here?	**Здесь есть телефон?** *Zdyes' yest' tilifon?*
May I have an ashtray?	**Можно пепельницу, пожалуйста?** *Mozhna pyepil'nitsoo pazhalsta?*
Could you bring me another glass / plate?	**Принесите, пожалуйста, ещё один стакан/тарелку?** *Priniseeti pazhalsta isho adeen stakan / taryelkoo?*
Could you change this fork / knife / spoon for me, please?	**Замените мне, пожалуйста, вилку/нож/ложку?** *Zamineeti mnye pazhalsta veelkoo / nozh / loshkoo?*
Can the heating be turned down / up?	**Можно понизить/повысить отопление?** *Mozhna paneezit' / paveesit' ataplyenye?*
Can the window be opened / closed?	**Можно открыть/закрыть окно?** *Mozhna atkreet' / zakreet' akno?*
I've stained my clothes, do have you any talcum powder?	**Я испачкался, у вас есть тальк?** *Ya ispachkalsya oo vas yest' tal'k?*
What time do you close?	**Во сколько вы закрываетесь?** *Va skol'ka vee zakreevaitis'?*
Can you call a taxi, please?	**Вызовете нам такси, пожалуйста** *Veezaviti nam taxee pazhalsta?*

Can we book a table for four?	**Можно заказать столик на четверых?** *Mozhna zakazat' stolik na chitvireekh?*
I'd like to book a table for two for this evening at eight/tomorrow evening in the name of …	**Я бы хотел заказать столик на двоих, на сегодня/на завтра на восемь вечера, на имя …** *Ya bee khatel zakazat' stolik na davaeekh, na sivodni/na zaftra na vosim' vyechira, na eemya*
Which day is closing day?	**Когда выходной день?** *Kagda veekhadnoi dyen'?*
What time does the restaurant open / close?	**Когда открывается/закрывается ресторан?** *Kagda atkreevaitsa / zakryvaitsa ristaran?*
I'd like to cancel a booking I made for this evening, for two people in the name of …	**Я бы хотел(а) аннулировать заказ на сегодняшний вечер, на двух человек, на имя …** *Ya bee khatyel(a) anooleeravat' zakas na sivodnyaschee vyechir, na dvookh chilavyek, na eemya …*
Is it necessary to book?	**Заказывать обязательно?** *Zakazyvat' abizatil'na?*

Is there a good restaurant in this area?	**Здесь есть хороший ресторан?** *Zdyes' yest' kharoshii ristaran?*
Is there a cheap restaurant near here?	**Здесь близко есть дешёвый ресторан?** *Zdyes' bleeska yest' dishovyi ristaran?*
Can you suggest a restaurant with typical local food?	**Вы можете мне указать ресторан с типичной кухней?** *Vee mozhiti mnye ookazat' ristaran s tipeechnai kookhnii?*
How do we get there?	**Как туда добраться?** *Kak tooda dabrat'sa?*
Excuse me, could you tell me where the ... Restaurant is?	**Извините, вы не знаете, где ресторан ...?** *Izveneeti vee nee znaiti gdye ristaran ...?*
What's is the best restaurant in town?	**Какой лучший ресторан города?** *Kakoi loocheei ristaran gorada?*
We would like to have a meal in an inexpensive restaurant	**Мы бы хотели пообедать в недорогом ресторане** *Mee bee khatyeli paabyedat' vnidaragom ristarani*

Is there a doctor here?	**Здесь есть врач?** *Zdyes' yest' vrach?*
Call a doctor / an ambulance!	**Вызовите врача/скорую помощь!** *Veezaviti vracha / skorooyoo pomash*
Go and get help, quick!	**Позовите на помощь, быстро!** *Pazaveeti na pomash beestra*
My wife is about to give birth	**Моя жена рожает** *Maya zhina razhayit*
Where is the nearest police station / hospital?	**Где отделение милиции/ ближайшая больница?** *Gdye addilyenye mileetsyi / blizhaishiaya bal'neetsa?*
I've lost my credit card / wallet	**Я потерял кредитную карточку/ бумажник** *Ya patiryal krideetnooyoo kartachkoo / boomazhnik*
I've lost my son / my bag	**Я потерял моего сына/мою сумку** *Ya patiryal mayevo seena / maioo soomkoo*
Fire!	**Пожар!** *Pazhar!*
Thief!	**Держи вора!** *Dirzhee vora!*

Are there any night clubs?	**Здесь есть ночные заведения?** *Zdyes' yest' nachneeye zavidyenya?*
Is there a good place / show for children?	**Здесь есть место/спектакль, подходящий для детей?** *Zdyes' yest' myesta / spiktakl padkhadyashyi dlya dityei?*
What's there to do in the evening?	**Что здесь можно делать вечером?** *Shto zdyes' mozhna dyelat' vyechiram?*
Where is there a cinema / a theater?	**Где здесь кино/театр?** *Gdye zdyes' kino / tyatr?*
Can you book tickets for us?	**Вы можете нам заказать билеты?** *Vy mozhity nam zakazat' bilyetee?*
Is there a swimming pool?	**Здесь есть бассейн?** *Zdyes' yest' baseyin?*
Are there any good excursions?	**Есть интересные экскурсии?** *Yest' intiryesnyi ekskoorsyi?*
Where can we play tennis / golf?	**Где можно поиграть в теннис/ в гольф?** *Gdye mozhna paigrat' ftennis / vgol'f?*
Can one go riding / fishing?	**Здесь можно покататься на лошади/порыбачить?** *Zdyes' mozhna pakatat'sa na loshadi / parybachit'?*

Good morning / afternoon	**Добрый день** *Dobreeyi dyen'*
Good evening	**Добрый вечер** *Dobreeyi vyechir*
Goodbye	**До свидания** *Dasvidanya*
See you soon!	**До скорого свидания!** *Daskorava svidanya!*
Pleased to meet you!	**Очень приятно!** *Ochin' pryatna*
How are you?	**Как дела?** *Kak dila?*
Well, thank you	**Спасибо, хорошо** *Spaseeba kharasho*
Please	**Пожалуйста** *Pazhalsta*
Excuse me	**Извините** *Izvineeti*
I'm sorry	**Мне очень жаль** *Mnye ochin' zhal'*
Thank you (very much)	**(Большое) спасибо** *(Bal'shoi) spaseeba*
Yes, please / No, thank you	**Да, спасибо/нет, спасибо** *Da spaseeba / nyet spaseeba*
I / We would like …	**Я бы хотел(а)/мы бы хотели…** *Ya bee khatyel(a) / mee bee khatyeli*

Things to remember

The typical food shop is called **Гастроном** *(gastronom) and is generally well supplied even though, strangely enough, many of the products are imported. Other shop signs to watch out for when you are shopping are* **Продукты** *(pradookti) or* **Кулинарий** *(koolinareei). In these shops, the goods are set out on large counters with assistants to supply you with what you want. They give you a ticket with the price of your shopping, you go to the till and pay, and return to pick up your purchase which will be given to you just as it is, regardless of weight or volume. Plastic shoppers (***пакеты***, pakyeti) are sold separately in a particular sector; don't forget to have the price included on the ticket.*

How much does a kilo/a hundred grams cost?	**Сколько стоит килограмм/ сто грамм?** *Skol'ka stoit kilagram / sto gram?*
How long does it keep?	**Сколько это может храниться?** *Skol'ka eta mozhit khraneetsa?*
I'll have this / that	**Я возьму это / то** *Ya vaz'moo eta / to*
I'd like two bottles	**Я бы хотел(а) две бутылки этого** *Ya bee khatyel(a) dvye booteelki etava*
Give me half a kilo	**Дайте мне пол кило этого** *Daiti mnye polkilo etava*
Could you pack it for the trip for me?	**Вы можете мне это завернуть в дорогу?** *Vee mozhiti mnye eta zavirnoot' vdarogoo?*
"Best by" date	**Срок годности** *Srok godnasti*

Russian grammar differs widely from English grammar. Here are some of the basic rules, to give you some idea of the structure of the Russian language.

Nouns may be: masculine, feminine and neuter. They are recognizable by their endings (except those nouns which finish in **ь**, which may be either masculine or feminine).

The nominative endings are as follows:

m: **consonant**		
й , ь	**дом, чай, день**	*dom, chai, dyen'*
f: **а, я, ь**	**книга, неделя, ночь**	*kneega, nidyelya, noch*
n: **о, ё, е**	**окно, бельё, море**	*akno, bilyo, morye*

The plural nominative endings are:

the vowels **а, я** become **ы, и**:

mother **мама**	mother **мамы**	*mama. mami*
nanny **няня**	nannies **няни**	*nyanya, nyani*

о, е become **а, я**:

letter **письмо**	letters **письма**	*pis, mo, pis, ma*
sea **море**	seas **моря**	*morye, marya*

Russian does not use definite and indefinite articles, so the word **дом** can be translated either as *the house* or as *a house*, according to the context.

Declensions are applied to nouns, adjectives and pronouns, which means that their endings change according to the role they play in the sentence, for instance, as subject: **the country** is big – **страна большая** (*strana bal'shaya);* object: I love the country – **я люблю страну** (*ya lyooblyoo*

stranoo). Besides the nominative and the accusative, the other cases are the genitive, the dative, the instrumental and the prepositional. This last is always preceded by prepositions, for example: **in the country** there are many people – **в стране много людей** (*fstranye mnoga lyoodeyi*).
If you wish to know all the endings you will have to consult a grammar book, but you should be able to make yourself understood by using words simply in the nominative, the subject case.

Adjectives are declined and agree with the noun to which they refer in number, gender and case. The nominative adjective endings are:
m: **ый, ий, ой**
f: **ая, яя**
nt: **ое, ее**

Only the masculine ending is indicated in our dictionary.

Adverbs generally finish in **о** and are invariable. They are normally formed from the adjective changing the ending **ый, ий** into **о**; for example: **good** – **хороший** (*kharoshii*) becomes **хорошо** (*kharasho*), so forming the adverb **well**.

Pronouns are also declined. Here they are in the nominative:

I	you	he	she	it	we	you (pl)	they
я	**ты**	**он**	**она**	**оно**	**мы**	**вы**	**они**
ya	*ti*	*on*	*ana*	*ano*	*mee*	*vee*	*anee*

The **ты** form of address is the familiar form corresponding to the French and Italian *tu*; the **вы** form is formal, French *vous* and Italian *lei*.

Verbs

Russian has only three tenses: present, past and future. However, all verbs have two aspects, the imperfective and the perfective. The imperfective is used when the action is not finished or is incomplete: I write, I'm writing, I was writing, I have written, I'll write. The perfective indicates that an action is concluded, over: I wrote, I will have written. Therefore the verbs with imperfective aspect have the present, the past and the future, while those with a perfective aspect have only the past and the future.
In the present tense, Russian verbs are conjugated according to the number and the person while in the past they have a single conjugation based on gender. So, a form exists for the masculine, one for the feminine, one for the neuter and a single form for the plural.
You will already have noticed how our examples indicate two endings, a masculine and a feminine ending: **я читал(а) книгу** (*ya chital/a kneegoo*) – **I was reading** a book.

Most of the verbs in the infinitive finish in **ать, ять** (first conjugation); or in **ить** (second conjugation). The regular verbs are conjugated as follows:

читать – to read (first conjugation) *chitat'*

present tense:

I read	**я чита-ю**	*ya chitayoo*
you read	**ты чита-ешь**	*tee chitaish*
he/she reads	**он/она чита-ет**	*on/ana chitait*
we read	**мы чита-ем**	*mee chitaim*
you read	**вы чтиа-ете**	*vee chitaiti*
they read	**они чита-ют**	*anee chitayoot*

past tense:

m:	**я, ты, он чита-л**	*ya, tee, on chital*
f:	**я, ты, она чита-ла**	*ya, tee, ana chitala*
m-f, pl:	**мы, вы, они чита-ли**	*mee, vee, anee chitali*

говорить – to speak (second conjugation) *gavareet'*

present tense:

I speak	**я говор-ю**	*ya gavaryoo*
you speak	**ты говор-ишь**	*tee gavareesh*
he/she speaks	**он/она говор-ит**	*on/ana gavareet*
we speak	**мы говор-им**	*mee gavareem*
you speak	**вы говор-ите**	*vee gavareety*
they speak	**они говор-ят**	*anee gavaryat*

past tense:

m:	**я, ты, он говор-ил**	*ya, tee, on gavareel*
f:	**я, ты, она говор-ила**	*ya, tee, ana gavareela*
m-f, pl:	**мы, вы, они говор-или**	*mee, vee, anee gavareely*

The verb **to be** is not used in the present, therefore **где дом?** (*gdye dom?*) means **where is the house?**
In the dictionary we have indicated the form of the imperfective infinitive: put the ending **ть** in place of those of the present and of the past (in the examples they are separated from the root by a hyphen) and you will make yourself clearly understood.

Verbs of movement
There are two different verbs of movement in Russian, both of which mean **to go**: **ходить/идти** (*khadeet'/itee*) which means to **go on foot**, and **ездить/ехать** (*yezdit' / yekhat'*) which means to **go in a vehicle**. Make sure you use the correct version when you ask the way.
Word order varies according to the meaning of the sentence.

Things to remember

After the suppression of the rather picturesque Soviet celebrations, not many holidays are left. The most important one is without any doubt New Year's Eve, while among the religious festivities Easter has pride of place in the Orthodox calendar, being of greater importance than Christmas.

New Year's Eve	**Новый год** *Novyi got*
March the eighth	**Восьмое марта** *Vas'moy marta*
Easter	**Пасха** *Paskha*
First of May	**Первое мая** *Pyervaee maia*
Victory Day (May 9)	**День победы** *Dyen pabyedi*
Christmas Eve	**Сочельник** *Sachel'nik*
Christmas Day	**Рождество** *Razhdistvo*

Things to remember

Hotel restaurants, as is usual in most countries, do not do justice to the variety and genuine nature of national cookery, offering uninteresting menus with little choice and frequently of mediocre quality. Luxury hotels generally give the preference to Western dishes and, apart from the impeccable service, gastronomic delights are somewhat lacking. Generally, full board is provided, but it is a good idea to choose to have at least one meal at the **шведский стол** *(shvyetski stol), the self-service buffet which normally provides an ample, excellent assortment of specialties.*

We've booked a room in the name of...	**Мы заказали номер на имя...** *Mee zakazali nomir na eemya...*
Can you have my luggage taken up?	**Можно отнести наверх мой багаж?** *Mozhna atnistee navyerkh moy bagazh?*
Can we have breakfast in our room at ...?	**Мы можем позавтракать в номере в...?** *Mee mozhim pazaftrakat' vnomiri v ...?*
May I have my key?	**Дайте мне мой ключ, пожалуйста?** *Daiti mnye moy klyooch pazhalsta?*
Put it on my bill	**Запишите это на мой счёт** *Zapisheeti eta na moy shot*
May I have another blanket / another pillow?	**Дайте мне, пожалуйста, ещё одно одеяло/ещё одну подушку?** *Daiti mnye pazhalsta isho adno adyalo /isho adnoo padooshkoo?*

I'd like to book a single / double room	**Я бы хотел(а) заказать одноместный/двухместный номер** *Ya bee khatyel(a) zakazat' adnamyesnyi / dvookhmyesnyi nomir*
I'd like a room with breakfast / one meal / full board	**Я бы хотел(а) номер с завтраком/с половиной пенсиона/с полным пенсионом** *Ya bee khatyel(a) nomir s zaftrakom / spalaveenai pinsyona/ spolnym pinsyonom*
How much is it per day / per week?	**Сколько это стоит в день/ в неделю?** *Skol'ka eta stoyt vdyen' / vnidyelyoo?*
Is breakfast included in the price?	**Завтрак включен в стоимость?** *Zaftrak fklyooshon fstoymast'?*
What time is breakfast / lunch / dinner?	**Во сколько завтрак/обед/ужин?** *Va skol'ka zaftrak / abyet / oozhin?*
We will be staying for three nights from ... until ...	**Мы остановимся на три ночи с ... до ...** *Mee astanovimsia na tree nochee s ... do ...*
We will get there at ...	**Мы приедем в ...** *Mee pryedim v ...*

Things to remember

*Today Russian cities are more or less one immense market. Things are bought and sold everywhere from mini-stalls consisting of a crate of fruit, to whole stadiums full of improvised vendors and enormous markets of knick-knacks and handicrafts on sale in the city parks. Tourists may be more interested in the picturesque aspect than in buying, but these places are certainly worth a visit. Likewise the covered fruit and vegetable markets where dogroses (***шиповник***, shipovnik) are to be found, bursting with vitamins and excellent for infusions, or* **клюква** *(klyookva), a delicious kind of myrtle rare in the West, or delicate gherkins and mushrooms in brine are sold. Moving southward from Russia, in the Caucasus and the Asiatic Republics, once Soviet States, markets become* **базар** *(bazars) full of exotic fragrances and fresh fruit, tastier and better than you ever dreamed.*

When is it market day in …?	**Какой день рынок в…?** *Kakoi dyen reenak v …?*
Until what time is the market open?	**До скольких работает рынок?** *Da skal'keekh rabotait reenak?*
Where do they sell cheese / fruit / spice?	**Где продают сыр/фрукты/специи?** *Gdye pradayoot sir / frookti / spyetsii?*
Please give me a hundred grams/ a kilo of …	**Дайте мне сто грамм/кило…** *Daiti mnye sto gram / kilo …*
I would like some raspberry / strawberry jam	**Дайте мне варенье из малины/ клубники** *Daiti mnye varyenye ees maleeni / kloobneeki*

Things to remember

The currency is the rouble, no longer divided into the legendary kopeks, which have been swallowed up in the whirlpool of inflation. Exchange offices are to be found more or less everywhere and the exchange rates can vary quite considerably (3-4%). The best rates are offered in the numerous kiosks set up in the streets or else at the exchange counters in shops; however, only dollars and marks are accepted; and worn bank-notes, or those issued more than twenty years ago are obstinately refused. Other European currencies can be changed in hotels and in many banks at rates which are perfectly in line with the international quotations.

I don't have enough money	**У меня не хватает денег** *Oo minya nikhvatait dyenik*
Do you have change?	**Вы можете мне разменять?** *Vee mozhiti mnye rasminyat'?*
Can you change a hundred thousand-rouble bank-note?	**Вы не разменяете сто тысяч рублей?** *Vee nirazminyaiti sto teesiach rublyei?*
I would like to change these pounds / dollars	**Я бы хотел обменять эти фунты (доллары)** *Ya bee khatyel(a) abminyat' eti foon-tee / dollari*
What is the exchange rate for dollars?	**Какой курс фунтд (доллара)?** *Kakoi kurs foon-teh dollara?*

0 **ноль**
nol'

1 **один**
adeen

2 **два**
dva

3 **три**
tree

4 **четыре**
chiteeri

5 **пять**
pyat

6 **шесть**
shest'

7 **семь**
syem

8 **восемь**
vosim

9 **девять**
dyevyat'

10 **десять**
dyesyat'

11 **одиннадцать**
adeenatsat'

12 **двенадцать**
dvinatsat'

13 **тринадцать**
trinatsat'

14 **четырнадцать**
chiteernatsat'

15 **пятнадцать**
pitnatsat'

16 **шестнадцать**
shisnatsat'

17 **семнадцать**
simnatsat'

18 **восемнадцать**
vasimnatsat'

19 **девятнадцать**
divyatnatsat'

20 **двадцать**
dvatsat'

21 **двадцать один**
dvatsat' adeen

22 **двадцать два**
dvatsat' dva

23 **двадцать три**
dvatsat' tree

30 **тридцать**
treetsat'

40 **сорок**
sorak

50 **пятьдесят**
pidisyat

60 **шестьдесят**
shisdisyat

70 **семьдесят**
syem'disyat

80 **восемьдесят**
vosimdisyat

90 **девяносто**
divyanosta

100 **сто**
sto

101 **сто один**
sto adeen

110 **сто десять**
sto dyesyat'

200 **двести**
dvyesti

300 **триста**
treesta

1000 **тысяча**
teesiacha

2000 **две тысячи**
dvye teesiacha

1.000.000 **миллион**
milyon

1st **первый**
pyervyi

2nd **второй**
ftaroi

3nd **третий**
tryetii

4th **четвёртый**
chitvyortyi

5th **пятый**
pyatyi

6th **шестой**
shistoi

7th **седьмой**
sid'moi

8th **восьмой**
vas'moi

9th **девятый**
vas'moi

10th **десятый**
disyatyi

Things to remember

> *Credit cards are accepted in hotels, the best restaurants and in some shops. Travelers cheques can be changed into roubles.*

How much does it cost?	**Сколько стоит?** *Skol'ka stoit?*
Can you bring me my bill, please?	**Принесите счёт, пожалуйста** *Priniseeti shot pazhalsta*
Can I pay by credit card?	**Можно платить кредитной карточкой?** *Mozhna plateet' krideetnai kartachkai?*
Do you take cheques / travelers' cheques?	**Вы принимаете чеки/ травеллерс чек?** *Vee prinimaiti cheki / traveller cheque?*
Could you give me the receipt, please?	**Дайте мне, пожалуйста, квитанцию?** *Daiti mnye pazhalsta kvitantsioo?*
Is service included?	**Обслуживание включено?** *Apsloozhivanye fklyoochino?*
Must I pay in advance?	**Нужно платить заранее?** *Noozhna plateet' zaranye?*
Must I leave a deposit?	**Нужно оставить аванс?** *Noozhna astavit' avans?*
I think you have given me the wrong change	**Мне кажется, вы неправильно сдали мне сдачу** *Mnye kazhitsa vee nipravil'na zdali mnye zdachoo*

Can you help me, please?	**Помогите мне пожалуйста?** *Pamageeti mnye pazhalsta?*
What's the matter?	**Что происходит?** *Shto praiskhodit?*
I need help	**Мне нужна помощь** *Mnye noozhna pomash*
I don't understand	**Я не понимаю** *Ya nipanimayoo*
Do you speak English?	**Вы говорите по-английски?** *Vee gavareeti paangleeiski?*
Can you repeat that, please?	**Повторите, пожалуйста?** *Paftareeti pazhalsta?*
I dont have any more money	**Я остался без денег** *Ya astalsa bis dyenik*
I can't find my son / my daughter	**Я не нахожу моего сына/мою дочь** *Ya ninakhazhoo mayevo seena / mayoo doch*
I am lost	**Я заблудился** *Ya zabloodeelsa*
Leave me alone!	**Оставь меня в покое!** *Astaf' minya fpakoi*

PRONUNCIATION 1

Cyrillic is a modified version of the Greek alphabet and is made up of 33 letters. In the table below, the second column gives the symbols used in the text to represent the English sound nearest to the Russian letter; the third column gives an example of an English word containing that sound.

LETTER		SYMBOL	PRONUNCIATION
А	а	*a*	as in pat
Б	б	*b*	
В	в	*v*	
Г	г	*g*	as in good
Д	д	*d*	
Е	е	*ye*	as in yes
Ё	ё	*yo*	as in the British yonder
Ж	ж	*zh*	as in pleasure, leisure
З	з	*z*	as in rose
И	и	*ee*	as in eel, complete
Й	й	*y*	as in you
К	к	*k*	as in clock
Л	л	*l*	
М	м	*m*	
Н	н	*n*	
О	о	*o or a*	as in stop in a stressed syllable as in lap in an unstressed syllable
П	п	*p*	
Р	р	*r*	
С	с	*s*	as in salt
Т	т	*t*	
У	у	*oo*	as in food
Ф	ф	*f*	
Х	х	*kh*	as in the Scottish Loch Ness
Ц	ц	*ts*	as in ants
Ч	ч	*ch*	as in child
Ш	ш	*sh*	as in shoot
Щ	щ	*sht*	as in finished

Ъ			(strong sound); unpronounced; it indicates a slight pause before the following sound
Ы	ы	*i*	as in ill
Ь		*'*	(weak sound); unpronounced; it softens the preceding consonant
Э	э	*e*	as in step
Ю	ю	*yoo*	as in you
Я	я	*ya*	as in yap

In our examples, the stressed syllable is clearly marked. The reason for this is that in Russian only the stressed vowels are pronounced strongly and clearly, while those that are unstressed all have a shorter, less distinct sound, particularly the **о**, **е**, **я**, which alter their pronunciation quite noticeably. The unaccented **о** is pronounced as a short **a**, for example:

молоко ***malako***, milk — **нога** ***naga***, leg

The unstressed **нога** and **я** sound much closer to the English **i** than to the **e**, and in any case are very short, for example:

можете ***mozhiti***, you can — **язык** ***izik***, tongue, language

In Russian, all consonants followed by the weak sound **ь** which we have marked with *a '* are pronounced with the tongue touching the palate, for example:

работать ***rabotat'***, to work — **итальянец** ***ital'yanits'***, Italian

In Russian, the voiced consonants (**б в д з ж г**) are pronounced like their unvoiced counterparts (**п ф т с ш к**) when followed by a voiced consonant or at the end of the word, for example:

друг ***drook*** friend — **завтра** ***zaftra*** tomorrow

Important!
In our pronunciation guide, we have tried to use the English letter(s) which most closely approximate the Russian sounds. Follow the symbols given, remembering that each one represents a sound, not a combination of letters.

Is it far?	**Это далеко?** *Eta daliko?*
Is it expensive?	**Это дорого?** *Eta doraga?*
Do you understand?	**Вы поняли?** *Vee ponyali?*
Can you help me?	**Вы можете мне помочь?** *Vy mozhity mnye pamoch?*
Where are the shops?	**Где магазины?** *Gdye magazeeni?*
How do I get there?	**Как туда проехать?** *Kak tooda prayekhat'?*
What's this?	**Что это?** *Shto eta?*

Things to remember

Imagine an enormous avenue with five or six lanes in each direction and wide sidewalks running in front of many stores with about ten shop windows each, and none of them looks in the least like a bar. It is a typical picture of suburban Moscow and there, if it is really urgent, you are in trouble. The public toilet in Russia is very rare, and in some cases it is outrageously dirty, even if a good number of pay-toilets have been opened downtown. It is not customary to ask in a **кафе** *(kafe) or a restaurant, but if a foreigner enquires, the request will generally be granted.*

Where is the restroom, please?	**Скажите пожалуйста, где туалет?** *Skazheeti pajalsta gdye tualyet?*
Is it a pay toilet?	**Туалет платный?** *Tualyet platnyi?*
There isn't toilet paper / soap	**Здесь нет туалетной бумаги/мыла** *Zdyes' nyet tualyetnai boomagi / meela*
Is there a toilet for the disabled?	**Здесь есть туалет для инвалидов?** *Zdyes' yest' tualyet dlya invaleedof?*
The toilet is blocked	**Унитаз засорён** *Oonitas zasaryon*

Things to remember

Smoking is generally not allowed in public places. "No smoking" is **не курить**! *(nye kooreet'). A fairly good selection of western brands of cigarettes of various origins are to be found at discount prices at roadside kiosks; you will pay much more for them in the hotels. Among the Russian brands, you should at least try the pestilential* **Беломор** *(byelamor), in flat, square cardboard packets, which bring back whiffs of the Five-Year-Plan era.*

Is smoking allowed here?	**Здесь можно курить?** *Zdyes' mozhna kooreet?*
Do you mind if I smoke?	**Вы не возражаете, если я закурю?** *Vee nivazrazhaeety yesli ya zakooryoo?*
May I have an ashtray?	**Можно пепельницу?** *Mozhna pyepil'nitsoo?*
Do you have any matches?	**У вас есть спички?** *Oo vas yest' speechky?*
Have you got a light?	**Огонька не найдётся?** *Agan'ka ninaidyotsa?*
Do you mind not smoking?	**Вы не могли бы перестать курить?** *Vee nimaglyi bee piristat' kooreet'?*
Can I offer you a cigarette?	**Можно вам предложить сигарету?** *Mozhna vam pridlazheet' sigaryetoo?*

Things to remember

Taxis abound, mainly old yellow or white Volga models, identified by the letter "T" on the doors. Don't be surprised at the number of private cars that stop to offer you a ride at a price, since the art of making ends meet is the prime mover of the post-Soviet economy. Be wary, however, unless you are with someone who knows his way around. Whether your vehicle is an authorized taxi or not, your fare should be agreed upon in advance.

Can you call a taxi for me, please?	**Вызовете мне такси, пожалуйста?** *Veezaviti mnye taxee pazhalsta?*
To the central station / airport	**На центральный вокзал/в аэропорт** *Na tsintral'nyi vagzal / vaeraport*
Take me to this address / to this hotel	**Отвезите меня по этому адресу/ в эту гостиницу** *Atvizeeti minya pa etamoo adrisoo / vetoo gasteenitsoo*
Is it far?	**Это далеко?** *Eta daliko?*
I am in a great hurry	**Я очень спешу** *Ya ochin' spishoo*
How much will it cost?	**Сколько это будет стоить?** *Skol'ka eta boodit stoit'?*
Stop here / round the corner	**Остановитесь здесь/за углом** *Astanaveetis' zdyes'/za ooglom*
Keep the change	**Сдачи не нужно** *Zdachi ni noozhna*

Things to remember

It is simple to telephone from hotels and private homes, either direct or through the operator. Public phones are more difficult; plastic tokens must be purchased from the subway stations or else they may occasionally be available at cigarette kiosks or newsstands. Phones taking phonecards are also present especially on the main streets of the big cities, in hotels, stations and airports, but they are run by several different companies, state-owned or private, each one competing with the others; consequently the phonecards that work in Moscow, for example, are not valid for St. Petersburg, and vice versa.

Is there a phone?	**Здесь есть телефон?** *Zdyes' yest' tilifon?*
Would you by any chance have a token?	**У вас не будет жетона?** *Oo vas niboodit zhetona?*
Do you sell phone tokens / phonecards?	**Вы продаёте жетоны/телефонные карточки?** *Vee nee pradayoti zhetoni / tilifonnyi kartachki?*
Can you give me a line?	**Вы можете меня соединить?** *Vee mozhiti minya saidineet'?*
I'd like to make a phone call	**Мне нужно позвонить** *Mnye noozhna pazvaneet'*
The number is …, room …	**Телефон номер …, комната …** *Tilifon nomir …, komnata …*

How much does it cost to call the United States/ the U.K.?	**Сколько стоит позвонить в Соединёиные штаты/ ВепикоБританию** *Skol'ka stoit pazvaneet' v init: saidineeo nieeshtatee/ vilikabritanya?*
I can't get a line	**Я не могу дозвониться** *Ya nimagoo dazvaneetsa*
The line is engaged	**Линия занята** *Leenya zanita*
Hello, this is ... speaking	**Алло, это ...** *Allo, eta ...*
May I speak to ... ?	**Позовите пожалуйста ...** *Pazaveeti pazhalsta ...?*
We've been cut off	**Меня прервали** *Minya prirvali*
Sorry, I've got the wrong number	**Извините, я не туда попал** *Izvineeti ya nitooda papal*
I can't hear very well	**Плохо слышно** *Plokha sleeshna*

YOU MAY HEAR:

Алло, кто говорит? *Allo kto gavareet?*	Hello, who's speaking?
Оставайтесь на связи *Astavaitis' na sviazi*	Hold the line
Его нет *Yevo nyet*	He isn't in
Вы не туда попали *Vee nitooda papali*	You have the wrong number

What time is it?	**Сколько сейчас времени?** *Skol'ka sichas vryemini?*
It is 1:00 A.M./P.M.	**Час дня/ночи** *Chas dnya / nochi*
It's two / three / four o'clock	**Два/три/четыре часа** *Dva /tree / chiteeri chasa*
8:00	**восемь часов** *Vosim' chasof*
8:05	**пять минут девятого** *pyat' minoot divyatava*
8:10	**десять минут девятого** *dyesyat' minoot divyatava*
8:15	**четверть девятого** *chetvirt' divyatava*
8:20	**двадцать минут девятого** *dvatsat' minoot divyatava*
8:30	**половина девятого** *palavina divyatava*
8:40	**без двадцати девять** *byes dvatsatee dyevyat'*
8:45	**без четверти девять** *byes chetvirti dyevyat'*
8:50	**без десяти девять** *byes disitee dyevyat'*

TIME 2

What time do you open / close?	**Во сколько открывается/ закрывается?** *Va skol'ka atkryvaitsa / zakryvaitsa?*
What time does the restaurant close?	**Во сколько закрывается ресторан?** *Va skol'ka zakryvaitsa ristaran?*
What time do the shops close?	**Во сколько закрываются магазины?** *Va skol'ka zakryvaiootsa magazeeni?*
How long will it take to get there?	**Сколько туда добираться?** *Skol'ka tooda dabirat'sa?*
We have arrived early / late	**Мы приехали рано/поздно** *Mee pryekhali rana / pozna*
It is early / late	**Сейчас рано/поздно** *Sichas rana / pozna*
What time does the bus leave?	**Во сколько уходит автобус?** *Va skol'ka ookhodit aftobus?*
The table is reserved for ... o'clock this evening	**Столик заказан на ... вечера** *Stolik zakazan na ... vyechira*
Midday	**Полдень** *Poldin'*
Midnight	**Полночь** *Polnach*

Things to remember

Even in new consumerist Russia, tips can open doors which would otherwise remain shut. In general perhaps , any service which is not apparently offered spontaneously can be "solicited" with more hope of success than in the West, without any moral misgivings. Tips in restaurants do no harm, obviously, but a well-placed tip in other places of entertainment can do wonders. And nowadays to make a good impression, you should be generous.

Should one give a tip?	**Принято ли давать на чай?** *Prineeta li davat' nachai?*
What tip does one give?	**Сколько мне дать на чай?** *Skol' ka mnye dat' nachai?*
I'm sorry, I have no small change	**К сожалению, у меня нет мелочи** *Ksazhalyenyoo oo minya nyet myelachi*
Keep the change	**Сдачи не надо** *Zdachi ninada*
Can you give me change for ... ?	**У вас есть сдача с ...?** *Oo vas yest' zdacha s ...?*

Half a liter of ...	**Поллитра ...** *Palleetra ...*
A liter of ...	**Литр ...** *Leetr ...*
A kilo of ...	**Кило ...** *Kilo ...*
Half a kilo of ...	**Полкило ...** *Palkilo*
A hundred grams of ...	**Сто грамм ...** *Sto gram ...*
A slice of ...	**Кусок ...** *Koosok ...*
A portion of ...	**Порция ...** *Portsya ...*
A dozen ...	**Дюжина ...** *Dyoozhina ...*

Gastronomic Dictionary

Russian - English

абрикос apricot
аванс deposit
август August
автобус bus
агенство agency
адрес address
Азербайджан Azerbaidjan
Азия Asia
азу see "National Dishes" p. 46
айва quince
Алиготе see "Wines" p. 31
алкоголь alcohol
алтайский сыр see "Cheeses" p. 21
алфавит alphabet
Америка America
американский *adj.* American
ананас pineapple
английский *adj.* English
Англия England
анис aniseed
анор ва пиез see "Dishes from the ex-Soviet States" p. 64
антрекот see "National Dishes" p. 46
апельсин orange
апрель April
аптека pharmacy
арахис peanut
арбуз watermelon
Армения Armenia
аромат aroma
артишок artichoke
аспирин aspirin
ассорти assortment
Аштарах see "Wines" p. 32
аэропорт airport

баба ромовая rum baba
бабушка grandmother
багаж baggage; **ручной багаж** hand baggage
базар market, bazar
базилик basil
баклажан eggplant
балет ballet
бальзам herb liqueur
балык see "Fish Starters" p. 14
банан banana
банк bank
банка jar, tin
бар bar
баран ram
баранина mutton
баранка ring cake
барбарис berberry
бассейн swimming pool
бастурма see "Dishes from the ex-Soviet States" p. 62
батон loaf
башня tower

безалкогольный non-alcoholic drink
безе meringue
бекас woodcock
Белоруссия Bielruss
белуга beluga
белый white; **белое вино** white wine
бензин gasoline
бензоколонка gas station
бефстроганов see "National Dishes" p. 46
билет ticket
бисквит 1) hard biscuit 2) sponge cake
биточки see "National Dishes" p. 46
бифштекс натуральный see "National Dishes" p. 46
бифштекс рубленый see "National Dishes" p. 46
блины see "Floury Fantasies" p. 23
блины с икрой see "Fish Starters" p. 14
блюдо dish (of food); **комплексные блюда** combination plates; **фирменное блюдо** house specialty
бобы broad beans
бог God
бок осетровый see "Fish Starters" p. 14
бокал tankard
болезнь illness
больница hospital
большой large
борщ see "National Dishes" p. 46 and "Dishes from the ex-Soviet States" p. 65
босбаш see"Dishes from the ex-Soviet States" p. 67
ботвинья see "National Dishes" p. 47
брак marriage
брат brother
бритва razor
брусника red bilberry
брынза see "Cheeses" p. 21
брюква rape
брюки trousers
буйвол buffalo
буква letter (of the alphabet)
булочка sandwich (may be sweet)
булочная breadshop
бульон see "The Basics" p. 41
бумага paper
бутерброд sandwich
бутылка bottle
буфет bar (in a cinema, theater etc.)
буханка loaf
быстро bistro

в in, at, to
в сметане see "Gastronomic Terms" p. 44
вагон carriage; **вагон-ресторан** dining car
валюта currency
ваниль vanilla
ванна bathroom
вареники see "Dishes from the ex-Soviet States" p. 66
варёный boiled
варенье see "Sweets" p. 36
варить to boil
ватрушки see "Floury Fantasies" p. 24
вафли wafer
ваш your
век century
вермишель noodles
вес weight
весы scales
ветчина see "Preserved Meats" p. 19
ветчино-рубленая колбаса see "Preserved Meats" p. 19
виза view
вилка fork
винегрет see "National Dishes" p. 47
вино wine; **белое вино** white wine; **игристое вино** sparkling wine; **красное вино** red wine; **креплёное вино** fortified wine; **полусухое вино** semi-sweet wine; **сладкое вино** sweet wine; **сухое вино** dry wine
виноград grapes
вишня wild cherry
включать to light
вкус taste, flavor
вкусный good, tasty
вода water; **минеральная вода** mineral water
водка see "Spirits" p. 27
воздух air
волжский сыр see "Cheeses" p. 22
волован puff pastry shell
волосы hair
вопрос question
воскресенье Sunday
восток east
врач doctor
время time
все all; **всё** everything
всегда always
встреча meeting
вторник Tuesday
второе блюдо main course
вход entrance
входить to go in
вчера yesterday
вы you (formal)

выбор choice, assortment
вылет departure (at airport)
вырезка жареная see "National Dishes" p. 47
высокий tall, high
выставка show, exhibition
выход exit
выходить to go out

газ gas
газета newspaper
газированный fizzy
галушки see "Dishes from the ex-Soviet States" p. 66
гамбургер hamburger
гардероб wardrobe
гарнир side dish, vegetable
гастроном food shop
гвоздика cloves
где where
главный main
глаз eye
глинтвейн see "Spirits" p. 28
глубокий deep
говорить to speak
говядина beef
говядина отварная с хреном see "National Dishes" p. 47
год year
голавль club
голландский сыр see "Cheeses" p. 22
голова head
голодный hungry
голос voice
голубой blue
голубцы see "Dishes from the ex-Soviet States" p. 66
голубь pigeon
гора mountain
горбуша see "Fish Starters" p. 14
горничная chamber maid
город city
горох peas; **турецкий горох** chick peas
горчица mustard
горький bitter
горячий hot, boiling
господин Mr, gentleman
госпожа Mrs, lady
гостиная lounge
гостиница hotel
гость guest
государство state
готовить to prepare, to cook
готовый ready
градус degree
гражданство nationality
грамм gram
гранат pomegranate
граница frontier
грейпфрут grapefruit

гренки see "Floury Fantasies" p. 24
греча maize
гречневая каша see "The Basics" p. 41
грецкий орех nut
грибы mushrooms; **белые грибы** boletus mushrooms
грибы в сметане see "National Dishes" p. 48
грибы солёные mushrooms in brine
грибной суп see "National Dishes" p. 47
грудинка see "Preserved Meats" p. 19
грудь breast
груздь milkman
Грузия Georgia
группа group
груша pear
грязный dirty
губа lip
гуляш see "National Dishes" p. 48
гусь goose
гусь жареный see "National Dishes" p. 48
гурджаани see "Wines" p. 32

да yes
давать to give
дама lady
дата date
дверь door
дворец building
девичьи слёзы see "National Dishes" p. 48
девушка girl
дедушка grandfather
дежурная floor service (hotel)
декабрь December
делать to do, to make
дело matter, business
день day
деньги money
дерево tree
держать to hold
десерт dessert
дети children
дешёвый cheap
джем jam (not homemade)
джин gin
диван sofa
диета diet
дикий wild
директор director, manager
дичь game (meats)
длинный long
для for
добрый good; **всего доброго** best wishes; **добро пожаловать!** welcome! **доброе утро** good

morning; **добрый день** hello
договор contract
дождь rain
доктор doctor
докторская колбаса see "Preserved Meats" p. 19
документ document
долгий long
доллар dollar
долька segment, piece, clove of
дом home
дома (at) home
домой (to) home
домашний see "Gastronomic Terms" p. 44
домашний сыр see "Cheeses" p. 22
дорога road, street
дорогой dear, expensive
дочь daughter
дрожжи yeast
друг friend
дуршлаг colander
духовка oven
душ shower
дым smoke
дыня melon
дядя uncle

Европа Europe; **Европейское Сообщество** European Community
его his; him
еда food
её her *(adj.); her (pron.);*
ежевика blackberry
ёрш ruff (fish)
если if
естественный natural
есть to eat

ж (on toilet door) ladies
жара heat; **жарко** it's hot
жареный see "Gastronomical Terms" p. 44
жарить to fry
жаркое see "The Basics" p. 41
жаркое из свинины с черносливом see "National Dishes" p. 48
жвачка chewing gum
желание wish
желе see "National Dishes" p. 49
желток yolk
жёлтый yellow
жена wife
женщина woman
жёсткий hard
живой alive; **живая рыба** fish sold live

живот stomach
животное animal
жидкий *adj.* liquid
жизнь life
жир fat (food content)
жирный *adj.* fat
жить to live
жульен see "National Dishes" p. 49
журнал magazine

за for, behind
заварка infusion
заварной boiled
завод factory
завтра tomorrow
завтрак breakfast
зад buttocks
задержка delay
зажигалка cigarette lighter
заказать to order
закон law
закрыто closed
закуски starter
зал hall; **банкетный зал** banquet hall
заливной see "Gastronomic Terms" p. 44
запад west
запас provisions
запах *noun* smell
запеканка see "The Basics" p. 41
запечённый see "Gastronomic Terms" p. 44
заяц hare
заяц тушёный в сметане see "National Dishes" p. 49
звать to call
меня зовут my name is
звезда star
звонок bell
здесь here
здоровый healthy; **на здоровье!** to your health!
здравствуйте! hello, hi
зелёный green
зелень aromatic herbs
земля ground, earth
земляника strawberry; **лесная земляника** wild strawberry
зеркало mirror
зерно grain
зефир see "Sweets" p. 36
зима winter
знакомый/ая m/f acquaintance
знать to know
золото gold
зонтик umbrella
зразы see "National Dishes" p. 49
зубатка sea bean
зубы teeth; **зубной врач** dentist

и and
игра game
идти to go
из see "Gastronomic Terms" p. 44
изучать to study
изюм sultanas
икона icon
икра see "Fish starters" p. 14 and Gastronomic Terms" p. 44
икра из баклажанов see "Dishes from the ex-Soviet States" p. 62
Икра кетовая see "Fish Starters" p. 16
Икра осетровая see "Fish Starters" p. 15
или or
имбирь ginger
иметь to have
имя name
индейка turkey
индекс zip code
инженер engineer
инжир fig
институт institute
интересный interesting
информация information
искуственный artificial
искусство art
история history, story
Италия Italy;
итальянец/нка *noun* Italian; **итальянский** *adj.* Italian
итог total
июль July
июнь June
их their; them

кабак tavern
кабан boar
кабаре cabaret
кабачки zucchini
кабачки фаршированные овощами see "National Dishes" p. 49
Каберне see "Wines" p. 32
Кавказ Caucasus
Кагор see "Wines" p. 32
каждый each
Казахстан Kazakhistan
какао cocoa
какой which
калач see "Floury Fantasies" p. 24
камбала sole
камбала "аврора" see "Dishes from the ex-Soviet States" p. 67
камень stone
канал canal
каперсы capers
каплун capon

капля drop
капуста cabbage;
брюссельская капуста Brussels sprouts
квашеная капуста sauerkraut
цветная капуста cauliflower
карандаш pencil
карась crucian carp
караси в сметане see "National Dishes" p. 50
карбонад see "Preserved Meats" p. 20
кардамон cardamom
карман pocket
карп carp
карп с красным вином see "National Dishes" p. 50
карта map
картина picture
карты playing cards
картофель potatoes
картофельные котлеты see "National Dishes" p. 50
картошка potatoes;
жареная картошка chips (UK), Frenchfries (USA)
касса cash-desk
кастрюля saucepan
кафе coffee-bar
кафетерий bar, caffetteria
качество quality
каша see "The Basics" p. 41
каштан chestnut; cabin
квартира apartment
квас see "Other Specialties" p. 39
квитанция receipt
кедр cedar
кедровый орешек pine nut
кекс see "Sweets" p. 36
кета dog salmon
кефаль mullet
кефир see "Other Specialties" p. 39
кизил cornelian cherry
кизлярка see "Spirits" p. 29
килограмм кг kilo
километр км kilometer
килька anchovy
Киндзмараули see "Wines" p. 32
кинза wild coriander
кинотеатр cinema
киоск kiosk
кисель see "National Dishes" p. 50
кислица wild sorrel
кислый acid, bitter
Китай China
клёцки see "Dishes from the ex-Soviet States" p. 66
клубника strawberry
клюква bog myrtle

ключ key
книга book
ковёр carpet
когда when
Кодры see "Wines" p. 32
кокос coconut
коктейль cocktail
кокурок see "Floury Fantasies" p. 24
колбаса see "Preserved Meats" p. 19
колготки tights
колесо wheel
количество quantity
кольцо ring
комиссионный магазин second-hand shop
коммунизм Communism
комната room
компот see "National Dishes" p. 50
конверт envelope
кондитерская cake shop
конец end
консервы preserves
конфеты candy, chocolates
конь horse
коньки skates
коньяк see "Spirits" p. 29
копчёный smoked
корабль ship
коренья herbs
корзиночка see "Sweets" p. 37
кориандр coriander
корица cinnamon
корова cow
короткий short
косточка stone (in a fruit)
кострец rump
кость bone
костюм dress
котлеты see "The Basics" p. 41
котлеты пожарские see "National Dishes" p. 51
котлеты по-киевски see "Dishes from the ex-Soviet States" p. 66
кофе coffee; **растворимый кофе** instant coffee
кофеварка coffee pot
кошелёк purse
кошка cat
крабы see "Fish Starters" p. 16
кран tap
крапива nettle
красивый beautiful
красный red
крахмал starch; **картофельный крахмал** potato flour
крем cream
Кремль Kremlin

крендель see "Floury Fantasies" p. 24
крепкий strong
кровать bed
кровь blood
кролик rabbit
круглый round
кружка tankard
крупа winnowed corn; **гречневая крупа** buck wheat; **манная крупа** semolina
крыжовник gooseberry
крыло wing
крыша roof
крышка lid
крюшон see "Spirits" p. 29
кто who
кукуруза maize
кулебяка see "Floury Fantasies" p. 24
кулинария bar, snack bar; **кулинарные изделия** prepared dishes
кулич see "Floury Fantasies" p. 24
культура culture
купаться to bathe
купе railway compartment
курага dried apricots
курить to smoke; **у нас не курят** no smoking
курица chicken; fowl
курица жареная в сухарях see "National Dishes" p. 51
курица под белым соусом see "National Dishes" p. 51
куропатка partridge
куропатки фаршированные see "National Dishes" p. 51
кусок piece, slice
кухня kitchen
кушать to eat

лавровый лист bay leaves
лагман see "Dishes from the ex-Soviet States" p. 64
лакрица licorice
лампа lamp
лангет see "National Dishes" p. 51
лапша see "National Dishes" p. 51
Латвия Latvia
латук lettuce
лево left
лёгкий light, easy
лёд Ice
леденец lollipop, candy
лекарство medicine
лепёшка flat, round bread
лес wood (small forest)
лестница stairs

лето summer
ливерная колбаса see "Preserved Meats" p. 20
Лидия молдавская see "Wines" p. 32
ликёр liqueur
лимон lemon
лимонная see "Spirits" p. 28
линь tench
лисичка chanterelle mushroom
лист sheet (of paper); leaf
Литва Lithuania
литр liter
лифт lift
лицо face
лобио see "Dishes from the ex-Soviet States" p. 62
лодка boat
ложечка teaspoon
ложка tablespoon
лоза vine
лосось see "Fish Starters" p.16
лук onion; **зелёный лук** chives; **лук-порей** leek
луна moon
лыжи ski
любительская колбаса see "Preserved Meats" p. 20
любовь love
люди people
люкс luxury
люля-кебаб see "Dishes from the ex-Soviet States" p. 67

м (on toilet door) men
магазин shop
май May
майка T-shirt
майонез mayonnaise
макароны see "National Dishes" p. 51
малина raspberry
маленький small
мало little
мальчик boy
мама mommy
мамалыга see "Dishes from the ex-Soviet States" p. 68
мандарин mandarin
манная каша see "The Basics" p. 41
манты see "Dishes from the ex-Soviet States" p. 64
маргарин margarine
маринованный marinated, pickled
марка postal stamp
мармелат soft fruit candy
март March
марципан see "Sweets" p. 37
маслята agaric mushrooms

маслины olives
масло butter, oil; **подсолнечное масло** sunflower seed oil; **растительное масло** vegetable oil; **сливочное масло** butter; **оливковое масло** olive oil
массаж massage
матрас mattress
мать mother
машина automobile
мебель furniture
мёд honey
медведь bear
медсестра nurse
между between, among
международный international
мелочь small change
меню menu
мера size
Мерло see "Wines" p. 33
место place
месяц month
метр м meter
метрдотель maitre d'hotel
метро М subway
мех fur; fur coat
милиция police
миллион million
миндаль almond
министерство ministry
минога lamprey
минута minute
мир 1) world; 2) peace
много much, a lot
мозг brain
можжевеловая see "Spirits" p. 28
можжевельник juniper
мой my
мокрый wet
молодой young, a young man
молоко milk; **обезжиренное молоко** skimmed milk; **сгущённое молоко** see "Sweets" p. 38; **сухое молоко** powdered milk; **цельное молоко** full cream milk
море sea
морковь carrot
мороженое see "Sweets" p. 37
морс see "Other Specialties" p. 39
Москва Moscow
московская колбаса see "Preserved Meats" p. 20
мост bridge
мотор engine
муж husband
музей museum
музыка music

мука flour
мускат muscatel
мускатный орех nutmeg
мусор garbage
мусс mousse
мы we
мыло soap
мягкий soft
мясное ассорти see "National Dishes" p. 52
мясо meat
мята mint

на to, for; **на чай** tip
навага navaga
наливка rosolio
налим burbot
Напареули see "Wines" p. 33
напиток drink; **спиртные напитки** drinks
Нарзан see "Other Specialties" p. 39
народ people
население population
настой infusion
настойка liqueur
наука science
начало beginning
начинка stuffing, filling
наш our
нашинковать to chop finely (vegetables)
не not
небо sky
неделя week
нежный tender
нерка red salmon
нет no
никто nobody
новый new **Новый год** New Year
нога leg, foot
нож knife
ножницы scissors
номер number, hotel room
нос nose
носки socks
ночь night
ноябрь November

обед dinner
окрошка see "National Dishes" p. 52
область region
обмен change
обслуживание service
обувь shoes
общество society
овёс oats
овощи vegetables
овсянка winnowed oats
огонь fire
огурец cucumber, gherkin
одежда clothes
одеяло blanket

океан ocean
окно window
окорок see “Preserved Meats” p. 20
октябрь October
окунь perch
окунь в молоке see “Dishes from the ex-Soviet States” p. 68
оладьи see “Floury Fantasies” p. 25
оливки olives
омар lobster
омлет see “National Dishes” p. 52
он he, him
она she, her
они they, them
опасный dangerous
оплата payment
опята nails
оранжевый orange (color)
орех nut
оружие weapon
осень autumn
осётр Russian sturgeon
осетрина see “Fish Starters” p. 16
оставлять to leave
остановка stop
осторожно! watch out!
острый hot (spicy)
отварной see “Gastronomic Terms” p. 44
ответ reply
отдел department, section
отдых rest
открытый open
откуда? where from?
отец father
офис office
официант/ка waiter, waitress
очень much
очередь queue, (in) order
очки glasses

палец finger
палтус turbot
пальто coat
памятник monument
папа daddy
папироса cigarette (with cardboard mouthpiece)
пара pair
парикмахерская hairdresser’s
парк park
партия (political) party
парфюмерия profumer-party
паспорт passport
паста paste; **зубная паста** toothpaste
пастернак parsnip
пастила see “Sweets” p. 37

Пасха Easter
патиссон pumpkin
патока molasses
пачка packet
паштет paté
пельмени see "National Dishes" p. 52
пенсия room and board
первый first; **первое блюдо** first course
переводчик translator
переговорный пункт (public) telephones
перепел quail
перерыв interval; **перерыв на обед** lunch break
переулок lane
перец bell peppers; **красный перец** chili; **чёрный перец** black pepper
персик peach
перцовка see "Spirits" p. 28
перчатки gloves
пескарь gudgeon
песня song
песок sand; **сахарный песох** icing sugar
Петра see "Wines" p. 33
петрушка parsley
печёнка liver
печёнка в сметане see "National Dishes" p. 52
печенье biscuit
печерица meadow mushroom
печь oven
пешеход pedestrian
пивная pub, tavern
пиво beer
пикули see "National Dishes" p. 53
пирог see "Floury Fantasies" p. 25
пирожки see "Floury Fantasies" p. 25
пирожное see "Sweets" p. 37
пирожное миндальное see "Sweets" p. 37
писатель writer
письмо letter; **заказное письмо** registered letter
питание nutrition
пити see "Dishes from the ex-Soviet States" p. 67
пить to drink
питевая вода drinking water
пиццерия pizzeria
пища food
пламя flame
пластырь Band Aid
платить to pay
платок handkerchief

платье dress, suit
плёнка film (for camera)
плечо shoulder
плита store
плов see "Dishes from the ex-Soviet States" p. 64
плод fruit
плохой bad
площадь square (in a town)
пляж beach
по see "Gastronomic Terms" p. 45
повар chef
повесть story
повидло see "Sweets" p. 37
погода weather
погреб cellar
подарок gift
подберёзовик brown boletus mushroom
подземный переход underpass
поднос tray
подосиновик red boletus mushroom
подушка cushion, pillow
поезд train
поездка trip
пожар fire
поздравить to wish (happy birthday, etc.)
покупка purchase
пол floor
пол- half-; **полкило** half a kilo
полено see "Sweets" p. 38
половина half
полотенце towel
полтавская колбаса see "Preserved Meats" p. 20
помидоры tomatoes
помощь help; **скорая помощь** ambulance
понедельник Monday
пончики see "Floury Fantasies" p. 25
порей leek
поросёнок заливной see "National Dishes" p. 53
поросёнок фаршированый гречневой кашей see "National Dishes" p. 53
порт port
портрет portrait
портфель ovenight bag
порция portion
порядок order
посадка landing (of a plane)
посол ambassador
постель bed
постный lean, without fat
посторонный stranger
посуда crockery
посылка packet, envelope

почта mail
почки kidneys
правда truth, justice
правило rule
право 1) (juridical) right; 2) right (not left)
православный orthodox
праздник holiday
прачечная laundry
предмет object
предприятие company, firm, business
президент president
привет greeting; **привет!** hello!
прилавок counter
прилёт arrivals (at the airport)
природа nature
приправа dressing (salad)
прихожая anteroom
причёска hair style
приятный pleasant
пробка cork, (bottle) top
программа program, show
продавец sales clerk (man)
продавщица sales clerk (woman)
продажа sale
продовольственный *adj.* food
продукт food product; **молочные продукты** *adj* dairy
прокат rental
Променисте see "Wines" p. 33
промышленность industry
пропуск pass (for an office)
проспект (main) road, street
простой simple
простокваша yoghurt
простыня sheet
просьба prayer, request
против opposite, contrary
профитроль profiterole dessert
профсоюз trade union
прощание goodbye, farewell
прямой straight
пряники see "Floury Fantasies" p. 25
пряность spices
Псоу see "Wines" p. 33
птичье молоко see "Sweets" p. 38
птица bird
пуб pub
пудинг pudding
пудра powder
путеводитель tourist guidebook
путешествие trip
путь road, way

пчела bee
пшеница corn
пшено maize
пюре purée see also "Gastronomic Terms" p. 45
пятница Friday

работа work
работать to work; **не работает** closed, out of order
рагу see "Gastronomic Terms" p. 45
рагу из овощей see "National Dishes" p. 53
Рагч иэ рчбца see «national Dishes" p. 53
радио radio
разговор conversation
размер measurement
разогреть to heat
район district, region
рак freshwater shrimp
раки натуральные see "Fish Starters" p.16
расписание timetable
распродажа sales
рассольник see "National Dishes" p. 53
расстегай see "Floury Fantasies" p. 26
расчёска comb
рафинад sugar cubes
ребёнок child
ревень rhubarb
редиска radish
редька wild radish
режиссёр (film) director
резать to cut
резервировать to reserve, to book
резина rubber
резус-фактор Rh factor; **положительный** positive; **отрицательный** negative
рейс N° flight number
реклама advertising
религия religion
ремонт *noun* repair
репа turnip
ресницы eyelash
республика republic
ресторан restaurant
рецепт recipe
Рим Rome
рис rice
рисовая каша see "The Basics" p. 41
Рислинг see "Wines" p. 33
рисовать to draw
Ркацители see "Wines" p. 33
рогалик brioche
родина native country
родители parents
родственник relation

Рождество Christmas
рожь rye
розмарин rosemary
розовый pink
рокфор roquefort
ром rum
роман novel
ромштекс see "National Dishes" p. 54
российский сыр see "Cheeses" p. 22
Россия Russia
рост stature
ростбиф see "National Dishes" p. 54
рубашка shirt
рубец tripe
рубленый chopped, minced
рубль rouble
рука hand, arm
рулет meat loaf
русский Russian
ручка pen
ручной *adj* manual; **ручной багаж** hand baggage
рыба fish
рыбное ассорти see "Fish Starters" p. 17
рыжик saffron milk cup mushroom
рынок market
рюмка small glass
рюмочная wine shop
рябина wild sorb
рябчик black partrdge
ряд order, line
ряженка see "Dishes from the ex-Soviet States" p. 67

с from, with
с яблоками see "Gastronomic Terms" p. 45
саго sago
сад garden
садиться to sit down
сазан carp
сайка sandwich (of white bread)
салат salad see "The Basics" p. 42 (for mixed salads see "National Dishes" p. 54-5) **зелёный салат** mixed wild salads
салат сузма see "Dishes from the ex-Soviet States" p. 65
сало lard
салфетка napkin
самовар samovar (for tea-making)
самогон see "Spirits" p. 29
самообслуживание self-service
самый the same, the most

сантиметр centimeter
сапог boot
сардельки see National Dishes" p. 56
сардины sardines
сахар sugar; **сахарная пудра** icing sugar; **сахарный песок** granulated sugar
сбитень see "Other Specialties" p. 39
свадьба wedding
свежий fresh
свёкла beetroot
свет light
светлый fair, blond
светофор traffic light
свеча candle
свидетель witness
свинина pork
свинья pig
свинушка agaric mushroom
свитер sweater
свободный free
святой holy
священник priest
сгущённое молоко see "Sweets" p. 38
сдача change money
сеанс show (at the cinema)
себя oneself; **на себя** pull; **от себя** push (on a door)
север north
северное сияние see "Spirits" p. 30
севрюга sevruga
сегодня today
сезон season
сейчас now
секретарь/ша secretary (man or woman)
секс sex
секунда second
селёдка herring
село village
сельдерей celery
сёмга see "Fish Starters" p. 17
семечки small seeds
семья family
семя seed
сентябрь September
сервелат see "Preserved Meats" p. 20
сердце heart
серебро silver
серый gray
серьги earrings
сестра sister
сиг see "Fish Starters" p. 17
сигарета cigarette
сидеть to sit
сидр cider
сила strength
синий blue

сироп syrup
система system
сказка fable
скатерть tablecloth
скидка discount
сковорода fryingpan
сколько how much, how many
скоро soon
скорость speed
скумбрия mackerel
слабый weak
славянский Slav
сладкий *adj.* sweet
слива plum
сливки cream; **взбитые сливки** whipped cream
словарь dictionary
слово word
сложный complex, complicated
сметана see "The Basics" p. 42
смех laughter
смородина currant; **красная смородина** redcurrant **чёрная смородина** blackcurrant
сморчок sponge
СНГ Community of Independent States
снег snow
снежки из яблок see "National Dishes" p. 56
собака dog
собор basilica
собрание meeting, assembly
собственность property
советовать to advise
советский Soviet
Советское Шампанское see "Wines" p. 33
Совиньон see "Wines" p. 34
сода soda
сок juice; **фруктовый сок** fruit juice
солёный salted, in brine
солонина salted meat
солнце sun
солённый salted
солёные грибы see "Other Specialties" p. 40
солёные овощи see "Other Specialties" p. 40
соль salt
солянка мясная see "National Dishes" p. 56
солянка рыбная see "National Dishes" p. 56
сом silurus; fish
сон 1) sleep 2) dream
сорочка shirt; **ночная сорочка** nightdress
сорт type, quality; **высший**

сорт best quality
сосиски see "National Dishes" p. 56
соус белый see "The Basics" p. 42
соус красный see "The Basics" p. 43
соус-хрен see "The Basics" p. 43
сохранять to preserve
союз union
спальня bedroom
спаржа asparagus
спасибо thank you
спать to sleep
спектакль show
специи spices
спина *noun* back
спирт alcohol
спиртные напитки alcoholic drinks
список list
спички matches
спорт sport
справка 1) information 2) certificate
справочник handbook, list
среда Wednesday
срочный urgent
СССР USSR
стадион stadium
стакан glass (for drinking)
старый old
стекло glass (the material)
стерлядь sterlet
сто hundred
стоимость cost
стоить to cost, to be worth
стол table
столица capital
столовая canteen, snack bar
сторона side, part
стоять to stand
страна nation
страхование insurance
стручки зелёной фасоли green beans
студент student
студень see "National Dishes" p. 56
стул chair
суббота Saturday
сувенир souvenir
судак perch
судак заливной see "National Dishes" p. 56
Судак по-польски see "National Dishes" p. 57
сумочка purse, handbag
суп (thick) soup
суп-пюре see "Gastronomic Terms" p. 45
суп-пюре из курицы see "National dishes" p. 57
суфле soufflé

сухари see “Floury Fantasies” p. 26
сухой dry; **сухое вино** dry wine; **сухой паёк** packed lunch
сушёный dried
схема scheme, figure
схема города city map
сцена scene
счастливый happy
счёт bill
США USA
сын son
сыр cheese
сырный салат see “National Dishes” p. 57
сырники see “Floury Fantasies” p. 26

табак tobacco
такси taxi; **стоянка такси** taxi stand
таможня customs
танец dance
тапочки slippers
тарелка plate
тариф fare, tariff
тархун see “Other Specialties” p. 40
татар *adj* Tartar
Твиши see “Wines” p. 34
твой your (informal, singular)
творог see “Cheeses” p. 22
театр theater
телевидение television
телеграмма telegram
телеграф telegraph
телёнок calf
телефон telephone
телятина veal
тёмный dark
температура temperature
тёплый warm, hot; **тепло** it's hot
тереть to grate
тёрка grater
термометр thermometer
тесто dough; **дрожжевое тесто** leavened dough; **песочное тесто** short pastry; **слоёное тесто** puff pastry
тетерев wood grouse
тетрадь copybook
тётя aunt
тефтели see “National Dishes” p. 57
тёша see “Fish Starters” p. 17
тишина silence
ткань cloth
тмин cummin
товар goods
товарищ companion
только only

томат-пюре tomato purée
томаты tomatoes
торговля trade
торжественный solemn
тормоза brakes
торт cake
торт "Прага" see "Sweets" p. 38
торт слоённый see "Sweets" p. 38
тост toast (when drinking)
трава herbs
трамвай tram
транспорт vehicle
треска cod
троллейбус trolleybus
труд work
трюфель truffles
туалет toilet
туман fog
тунец tunafish
турист/ка tourist
тут here
тутовка see "Spirits" p. 30
тутовник mulberry
туфли shoes
тушёный see "Gastronomic Terms" p. 45
ты you (informal, singular)
тыква pumpkin

углеводы carbohydrates
угличеcкий сыр see "Cheeses" p. 22
угол angle; corner
уголь coal
угорь eel
ужин supper
Узбекистан Uzbekistan
укроп dill
Украйна Ukraine
украшение decoration
уксус vinegar
улица street, road
уметь to be able
умный intelligent
универмаг department stores
университет university
упаковка packing
урожай harvest
урок lesson
устрицы oysters
утка duck
утка жареная в винном соусе see "National Dishes" p. 57
утро morning
утюг iron (for clothes)
уха see "National Dishes" p. 57
ухо ear
учитель master
уютный comfortable

фазан pheasant

факс fax
фамилия surname
фарфор porcelain
фаршированный stuffed, filled
фаршированная щука see "National Dishes" p. 58
фасоль beans
фасолевый суп see "National Dishes" p. 58
февраль February
фейхоа fei-hoy (chinese fruit)
фен hair dryer
Фетяска see "Wines" p. 34
фига fig
филе see "National Dishes" p. 58
филе рыбное fish fillet
филиал agency
фильм film
финик date (the fruit)
фирма company, business
фирменный *adj.* house; **фирменное блюдо** specialty of this place
фисташки pistachio
фольга tin foil
фонтан fountain
форель trout
форма shape
форшмак see "National Dishes" p. 58
фотография photograph
Франция France
фрикадельки meatballs
фрукты fruits
фундук hazelnut
фуниколёр cable railway
фрукты fruits

халва see "Sweets" p. 38
харчо see Dishes of the ex-Soviet States" p. 62
хачапури see "Floury Fantasies" p. 26
Хванчкара see "Wines" p. 34
хворост see "Floury Fantasies" p. 26
хвост tail end, queue
херес sherry
химчистка dry cleaning
хлеб bread; **белый хлеб** white bread; **чёрный хлеб** black bread
хлопок cotton
ходить to go on foot, to walk
холодец see "National Dishes" p. 58
холодильник refrigerator
холодный *adj.* cold; **холодно** It's cold
хороший good
хозяин owner

хрен horseradish
хрусталь crystal
художник artist
хурма persimmon

царь tsar
цвет color
цветы flowers
цедра dried citrus peel
цена price
центр center
церковь church
цесарка guinea fowl
цикорий chicory
Цинандали see "Wines" p. 34
цирк circus
цитрон citron
цукат candied fruit
Цымлянское игристое see "Wines" p. 34
цыплёнок spring chicken
цыплёнок табака see "Dishes from the ex-Soviet States" p. 62
цыплята жареные see "National Dishes" p. 58

чабёр savory
чавыча royal salmon
чай tea
чайник teapot
час now
частный private
чача see "Spirits" p. 30
чашка cup
чашечка coffee cup
чебуреки see "Floury Fantasies" p. 26
чеддар cheddar
чек check, receipt
человек man, person; **молодой человек** young man
чемодан suitcase
черешня cherries
черника bilberry
чернослив prunes
чёрный black
Чёрный доктор see "Wines" p. 35
чеснок garlic
чехохбили see "Dishes from the ex-Soviet States" p. 62
чечевица lentils
Чечня Checheno-Ingush Republic
число number, date
чистый clean
читать to read
чихиртма see "Dishes from the ex-Soviet States" p. 63
что what
чулки stockings

шампанское champagne, sparkling wine
шампиньон cultivated mushroom
шампунь shampoo
шахматы chess
шашлык see "The Basics p. 43 and "Dishes from the ex-Soviet States" p. 63
шашлык из осетрины see "National Dishes" p. 58
Шашлык иэ угря see "National Dishes" p. 59
шёлк silk
Шемах see "Wines" p. 35
шерсть wool
шеф chef
шина tire
школа school
шницель see "National Dishes" p. 59
шоколад chocolate, hot chocolate
шоколадка (bar of) chocolate
шафран saffron
шведский стол restaurant service
швейцарский сыр Swiss gruyère
шофёр driver
шпик lard
шпинат spinach
шпроты anchovies
штопор corkscrew
шуба fur
шутка joke

щавель sorrel
щётка brush
щи see "National Dishes" p. 59
щука luce;
фаршированная щука see "National Dishes" p. 58

экзамен examination
эклер see "Sweets" p. 38
экскурсия trip, excursion
электрический electric
электробритва electric razor
Эрмитаж Hermitage
эскалоп see "National Dishes" p. 59
Эстония Esthonia
эстрагон tarragon
этаж floor
этот/эта/это this

юг south
Южнобережный see "Wines" p. 35
юность youth

я I (pron.)

яблоко apple
ягоды berries
ягоды со взбитыми сливками see "National Dishes" p. 60
ядовитый poisonous
язык tongue, language
язык отварной see "National Dishes" p. 60
ячмень barley
яичница see "National Dishes" p. 60; **взбитая яичница** scrambled eggs; **яичница глазунья** fried egg
яйцо egg; **яйцо всмятку** boiled egg
яйцо вкрутую hard-boiled egg
яйца фаршированные икрой see "Fish Starters" p. 18
январь January
Ясман-Салик see "Wines" p. 35
яства delicacies

English - Russian

à la carte бумага *boomaga;* **à la** по меню *paminyoo*
above над *nat*
acid кислый *keeslyi*
acidulous недозрелый *nidazryelyi*
acquaintance знакомый *znakomyi*
additive указатель *ookazatil'*
address адрес *adryes*
adult взрослый *vzroslyi*
(to) **advise** предупреждать *pridooprizhdat'*
Africa африка *afrika*
after потом *patom*
afternoon snack полдник *polnik*
again ещё *isho*
against против *protif*
agarics маслята *maslyata*
aged выдержанный *veedirzhanyi*
ahead вперёд *fpiriot*
air воздух *vosdookh;* **air conditioning** кондиционер *kanditsyanyer*
airport аэропорт *aeraport*
alarm clock будильник *boodeel'nik*
alcoholic алкагольный *alkgol'nyi*
alcoholic drinks алкагольные напитки *alkagol'nyi napeetki*
all всё *fsyo*
almonds миндаль *mindal'*
almost почти *pachtee*
alone одинокий *adinokii*
also тоже *tozhe*
always всегда *sfyegda*
America Америка *amierika*
American американский *amirikanskii*
anchovy килька *keel'ka*
and и *ee*
aniseed анис *anees*
(to) **answer** отвечать *atvyechat'*
antibiotic антибиотик *antibiotic*
any любой *lyooboi*
aperitif аперитив *apiriteef*
appetite апетит *apitit;* **bon appétit** приятного апетита *pryatnava apiteeta*
apple яблоко *iablaka*
appointment встреча *fstryecha*
apricot абрикос *abrikos*
April апрель *apryel*
aroma аромат *aramat*
aromatic ароматический *aramateechiskii*
aromatic herbs зелень *zyelin'*

around вокруг *vakrook*
around окрестности *akryestnasti*
(to) **arrive** приехать *priiekhat'*
artichoke артишок *artishok*
ash пепел *pyepyel*
ashtray пепельница *pyepil'nitsa*
Asia Азия *aziia*
(to) **ask** спросить *spraseet'*
asparagus спаржа *sparzha*
aspirin аспирин *aspireen*
at least по крайней мере *pakrainii myeri*
August август *afgoost*
Australia Австралия *afstralya*
Austria Австрия *afstria*
Austrian австрийский *afstreeskii*
authentic подлинный *podlinyi*
(to) **avoid** избегать *izbigat'*

back *adv* назад *nazat*
bacon грудинка *groodeenka;* **smoked bacon** копчёная грудинка *kapchonaya groodeenka*
bad плохой *plakhoi*
bag сумка *soomka*
banana банан *banan*
bank банк *bank*
bar бар *bar*
barley ячмень *ichmyen'*
barman бармэн *barmen*
basil базилик *bazeelik*
bass *(fish)* зубатка *zoobatka*
Bavarian баварский *bavarskii*
bay лавровый лист *lavrovyi list*
(to) **be** быть *beet'*
(to) **be sufficient** хватать *khvatat'*
beans фасоль *fasol'*
beautiful красивый *kraseevyi*
bed постель *pastyel'*
beef говядина *gavyadina*
beer пиво *peeva;* **light beer** светлое пиво *svyetlaye peeva; peeva vrazleef;* **small beer** маленькая кружка пива **draught beer** пиво вразилв *peeva vrah-sleef;* **large beer** большая кружка пива *bal'shaya krooshka peeva*
beetroot свёкла *svyokla*
before *adv* раньше *ran'she*
beginning начало *nachala*
behind сзади *zadi*
berry ягода *yagada*
beside рядом *ryadam*

better *adj* лучший *loochshii*
better *adv* лучше *loochshe*
between через *cheris*
big большой *bal'shoi*
bill счёт *shot*
bird птица *pteetsa*
biro ручка *roochka*
biscuits печенье *pichyenye*
(to) **bite** кусать *koosat'*
bitter *adj* горький *gor'kii; noun* горькая настойка *gor'kaya nastoika*
black currant смородина *smarodina*
black чёрный *chornyi*
blackberry ежевика *izhiveeka*
blood кровь *krof'*
blueberries черника *chirneeka*
(to) **boil** варить *vareet'*
boiled варёный *varyonyi*
boiled варёный *varyonyi;* **(boiled meats)** мясо отварное *myasa atvarnonye*
boiling кипящий *kipyashii*
boletus mushrooms белые грибы *byelyi gribee*
Bologna Болонья *bolonya*
bone кость *kost'*
(to) **book** заказать *zakazat'*
book книга *kneega*
booking заказ *zakas*
boots сапоги *sapagee*
bottle бутылка *booteelka*
bottle opener штопор *shtopar*
bottled бутылочный *booteelachnyi*
bovine рогатый скот *ragatyi skot*
box коробка *karopka*
boy мальчик *mal'chik*
brain мозг *mosk*
bread хлеб *khlyep;* **sponge-cake** бисквит *biskveet*
bread-sticks соломка (печенье) *salomka (pichenye)*
breadcrumbs панировочные сухари *panirovachnye sookharee*
(to) **break** разбить *razbeet'*
breakdown поломка *palomka*
breakfast завтрак *zaftrak*
breast грудь *groot'*
bring, take, carry носить *naseet'*
brioche рогалик *ragalik*
broad beans бобы *babee*
broken сломаный *slomanyi*
broth бульон *boolyon*
browned поджаренный *padzharinyi*

brush щётка *shotka*
Brussels sprouts брюссельская капуста *bryoosyel'skaya kapoosta*
buds, sprouts побеги *pabyegi*
buffalo буйвол *booival*
bun, scone лепёшка *lipyoshka*
(to) **burn** жечь *zhyech*
burnt жжёный *zhzhonyi*
bus автобус *aftoboos*
butcher's мясной магазин *myasnoi magazeen*
butter масло *masla*
buttered намазанный маслом *namazanyi maslam*
button пуговица *poogavitsa*
(to) **buy** купить *koopeet'*

cabbage капуста *kapoosta*
cacao какао *kakao*
cake shop кондитерская *kandeeterskaya*
cake, sweet торт *tort*
calamary кальмары *kal'mary*
(to) **call** звать *zvat'*
call (phone call) звонок *zvanok*
calm спокойый *spakoinyi*
calorie калория *kaloria*
camomile валерьянка *valirìyanka*
canapé тартинки *tarteenki*
(to) **cancel (a flight)** отменить *atmineet'*
candied fruits цукаты *tsookati*
candle свеча *svicha*
candy карамель *karamyel'*
canopener открывалка *atkreevalka*
capers каперсы *kapirsi*
car park стоянка *stayanka*
carafe, decanter графин *grafeen*
caramel жжёный сахар *zhzhonyi sakhar*
careful внимательный *vnimatil'nyi*
carrot морковь *markof'*
cartcereals злаки *zlaki*
cash desk касса *kasa*
cash наличные *naleechnyi*; **in cash** наличными *naleechneemi*
cashier кассир *kaseer*
casserole кастрюля *kastryoolya*
cauliflower цветная капуста *tsvitnaya kapoosta*
caviar икра *ikra*
celery сельдерей *sil'direi*
cellar погреб *pogrip*

center центр *tsentr*
central центральный *tsintral'nyi*
chair стул *stool*
champagne шампанское *shampanskaye*
(to) **change** менять *minyat'*
change сдача *zdacha*
change обмен *abmyen;* **Exchange office** обмен валюты *abmyen valyooti*
(to) **check, control** контролировать *kantraleeravat'*
check чек *chek*
cheerfulness веселье *visyelye*
cheese сыр *sir*
cherry черешня *chiryeshnya*
chestnut каштан *kashtan*
chestnuts каштаны *kashtany*
(to) **chew** жевать *zhivat'*
chick peas турецкий горох *tooryetskii garokh*
chicken курица *kooritsa*
chicory цикорий *tsikori*
child ребёнок *ribyonak*
chili красный перец *krasnyi pyerits*
chitterlings потроха *patrakha*
chocolate шоколоад *shakalat*
chocolates шоколадные конфеты *shakaladnyi kanfyeti*
chop жареное мясо *zharinaye myasa*
chop, cutlet отбивная *atbivnaya*
Christmas Рождество *razhdistvo*
cigar сигара *sigara*
cigarette сигарета *sigaryeta*
cinnamon корица *kareetsa*
citron кедр *kyedr*
citrus цитрусовое *tsitroosavaye*
city город *gorat*
clean чистый *cheestyi*
clear светлый *svyetlyi*
client, customer клиент *klyent*
cloakroom гардероб *gardirop*
(to) **close** закрыть *zakreet'*
closed закрытый *zakreetyi*
closing закрытие *zakreetye*
cloud облако *oblaka*
coat пальто *pal'to*
Coca Cola Кока-Кола *koka-kola*
cockles песчанка *pishanka*
coconut какос *kakos*
cod треска *triska*

coffee кофе *kofi;* **American coffee** жидкий кофе *zhitkezh kofi;* **Expresso coffee** кофе эспрессо *kofi espresso*
coin монета *manyeta*
cold *adj* холодный *khalodnyi*
color цвет *tsvyet*
coloring красители *kraseetili*
(to) **come** прийти *priitee*
comfortable удобный *oodobnyi*
communication общение *apshyenye*
complaint жалоба *zhalaba*
compulsory обязательный *abizatyel'nyi*
cone (ice-cream) трубочка *troobachka*
(to) **confirm** утверждать *ootvirzhdat'*
(to) **continue** продолжать *pradalzhat'*
(to) **cook** готовить *gatovit'*
cook повар *povar*
cooked: well cooked зажаренный *zazharinyi;* **cooked just right** средней зажаренности *sryednii zazharinasti;* **rare, underdone** с кровью *skrovyoo*
cookies печенье *pichyenye*
cooking time варка *varka*
cool свежий *svyezhii*
(to) **cool** охлаждать *akhlazhdat'*
cork пробка *propka*
corn пшеница *pshineetsa*
corner угол *oogal*
(to) **cost** стоить *stoit'*
cost цена *tsina*
cotton хлопок *khlopak*
country страна *strana*
country деревня *diryevnya*
(to) **cover** покрывать *pakreevat'*
cow корова *karova*
crab краб *krap*
crayfish рак *rak*
cream сливки *sleefki;* **sour cream** сметана *smitana;* **whipped cream** взбитые сливки *vzbeetyi sleefki*
cream puff пончик *ponchik*
cream крем *krem*
credit card кредитная карта *krideetnaya karta*
crisps хрустящий картофель *khroostyashii kartofyel'*
croquette крокетка *krakyetka*
crouton гренки *gryenki*

crowded переполненный *piripolninyi*
crunchy хрустящий *khroostyashii*
crust корка *korka*
crustacean ракообразные *rakabraznyi*
cube кубик *koobik*
cube кусочек *koosochek;* **ice cube** кусочек льда *koosochek l'da*
cucumber, gherkin огурец *agooryets*
cummin тмин *tmeen*
cup бокал *bakal*
cup чашка *chashka;* **coffee cup** чашечка *chashechka*
currency валюта *valyoota*
current *adj.* текущий *tikooschii*
cushion подушка *padooshka*
custodian сторож *storash*
(to) **cut** резать *ryezat'*
cutlery приборы *pribori*
cutlet отбивная котлета *atbivnaya katlyeta*

damp влажный *vlazhnyi*
(to) **dance** танцевать *tantsivat'*
dark тёмный *tyomnyi*
dates (fruit) финики *feeniki*
daughter дочь *doch'*
day день *dyen'*
dear дорогой *daragoi*
December декабрь *dikabr'*
decorated украшенный *ookrasheenyi*
decoration украшение *ookrashenye*
delay задержка *zadyershka*
dentex кривозуб *krivazoop*
denture зубной протез *zoobnoi prates*
(to) **deposit** отдавать на хранение *atdavat'na khranyenye*
dessert десерт *disert*
devil дьявол *dyaval*
diabetic диабетический *diabiteechiskii*
diet диета *dyeta*
different другой *droogoi*
difficult трудный *troodnyi*
digestible удобоваримый *oodobavareemyi*
digestive способствующий пищеварению *spasopstvooyooschii pishivaryenyoo*
dinner обед *abyet*
directions указания *ookazanya*
dirty грязный *gryaznyi*
disabled инвалид *ivaleet*

discotheque дискотека *diskatyeka*
dish (of food) блюдо *blyooda*
dish блюдо *blyooda;* **(plate)** тарелка *taryelka*
(to) **disinfect** дизинфецировать *dizinfitseeravat'*
distance расстояние *rastayanye*
distributing machine автомат *aftamat*
(to) **disturb** мешать *mishat'*
doctor врач *vrach*
documents документы *dakoomyenti*
dollars доллары *dolari*
(to) **do,** (to) **make** делать *dyelat'*
door дверь *dvyer'*
double двойной *dvainoi*
dough тесто *tyesta;* **(Italian) pasta** макароны *makarony;* **short pastry** песочное тесто *pisochnaye tyesta;* **puff pastry** слоёное тесто *slayonaye tyesta*
down внизу *vnizoo*
dressing (salad) приправа *priprava*
(to) **drink** пить *pit'*
drink напиток *napeetak*
drunk пьяный *pianyi*
dry сухой *sookhoi*
duck утка *ootka*
Dutch голландский *galanskii*
duty долг *dolk*

each каждый *kazhdyi*
ear ухо *ookha*
early fruits/vegetables первинки *pierveenki*
early, soon скоро *skora*
east восток *vastok*
Easter Пасха *paskha*
easy лёгкий *liokhkii*
(to) **eat** есть *yest'*
economic дешёвый *dishovyi*
EEC ээс *yees*
eel угорь *oogar*
egg plant баклажаны *baklazhani*
egg white белок *bilok*
egg яйцо *iitso*
electricity электричество *iliktreechistva*
embassy посольство *pasol'stva*
empty пустой *poostoi*
end конец *kanyets*
endive эндивий *endeevii*
England Англия *anglya*
English английский *anglieeskii*

enough достаточно *dastatachna*
entrance вход *fkhot*
(to) **enter** войти *vaitee*
envelope конверт *kanvyert;* **(shopper)** пакет *pakyet*
escalop эскалоп *eskalop*
Europe Зврпа *yevropa*
evening вечер *vyechir*
except кроме *kromi*
excursion экскурсия *ikskoorsya*
exit выход *veekhat*
expensive дорогой *daragoi*
expert *adj* опытный *opeetnyi; noun* эксперт *ekspyert*
express *noun* экспресс *ekspres*
external внешний *vnyeshnii*
extract экстракт *ekstrakt*
eye глаз *glas*

(to) **fall** упасть *oopast'*
fainted без сознания *byessaznanya*
family семья *simya*
famous известный *izvyesnyi*
far далеко *daliko*
farm разведение *razvidyenye*
farmer крестьянин *kristyanin*
fast *adj* быстрый *beestryi*
fast *adv* быстро *beestra*
fat *noun* жир *zhir; adj* жирный *zheernyi*
favor одолжение *odalzhyenye*
February февраль *fivral'*
(to) **feel** чувствовать *choostvavat'*
feet ноги *nogi;* **on foot** пешком *pishkom*
fig инжир *inzheer*
fillet филе *file*
(to) **filter** процедить *pratsideet'*
(to) **find** найти *naeeti*
(to) **finish** заканчиваь *zakanchivat'*
fire огонь *agon'*
first первый *pyervyi*
fish рыба *reeba*
fishing рыбалка *reebalka*
fizzy газированный *gaziirovanyi*
flakes хлопья *khlopya*
flame пламя *plamya*
flask фиаско *fiasco*
flat плоский *ploskii*
(to) **flavor** приправить *pripravit'*
flavor вкус *fkoos*
flesh, pulp мякоть *myakat'*

flight number рейс № *ryeis nomir*
floor этаж *etazh*
flour мука *mooka*
flowers цветы *tsvyee eh-tee*
fly муха *mookha*
food cooked on a spit шашлык *shashleek*
food питание *pitanye*
food poisoning пищевое отравление *pishivoye atravlyenye*
foodstuffs продукты *pradookty*
for для *dlya*
foreign иностранный *instranyi*
(to) **forget** забыть *zabeet'*
fork вилка *veelka*
fowl курица *kooritsa*
France Франция *frantsya*
free (without payment) бесплатный *bisplatnyi*
free свободный *svabodnyi*
French *adj* французский *frantsooskii*
Friday пятница *pyatnitsa*
fried жареный *zharyenyi*
fried food жареное кушанье *zharinaye kooshanye*
friend друг *drook*
fritters блинчики *bleenchiki*
frog лягушка *ligooshka*
frozen замороженный *zamarozhinyi*
fruit фрукты *frookty*
fruit juice сок *sok*
fruit salad фруктовый салат *frooktovyi salat*
frying pan сковорода *skavarada*
full полный *polnyi*
full-flavored (of wine) плотный *plotnyi*

game (meats) дичь *dich*
garden сад *sat*
garlic чеснок *chisnok*
gas газ *gas*
gelatine желатин *zhilateen*
German немецкий *nimyetskii*
Germany Германия *germanya*
gift подарок *padarak*
ginger тыква *tikeve*
girl девушка *dyevooshka*
(to) **give** дать *dat'*
glass стакан *stakan*
glass стекло *stiklo*
glasses очки *achkee*
(to) **glaze** глазировать *glazeeravat'*

gloves перчатки *pirchatki*
(to) **go (on foot)** идти *itee;* **(in a vehicle)** ехать *yekhat'*
(to) **go down** спускаться *spooskat'ka*
(to) **go out** выходить *veekhad'eet*
(to) **go up** подниматься *padnimat'sa*
gold золото *zolata*
golden позолоченный *pazalochinyi*
good хороший *kharoshii;* **(of food)** вкусный *fkoosnyi*
goose гусь *goos*
grain зерно *zirno*
grandfather дедушка *dyedooshka*
grandmother бабушка *babooshka*
grapefruit грейпфрут *greipfroot*
grapes виноград *vinagrat*
grated тёртый *tyortyi*
greasy смазанный маслом *smazanyi maslam*
Great Britain Великобритания *vilikabritanya*
Greece Греция *gryetsya*
Greek *adj* греческий *gryechiskii*
green beans стручковая фасоль *stroochkovaya fasol'*
green зелёный *zilionyi*
greens овощи *ovashi*
grill решётка *rishotka*
group группа *groopa*
guide гид *git*
guinea fowl цесарка *tsesarka*

half половина *palaveena* *noun* средство *sryetstva*
ham ветчина *vichina*
hand рука *rooka*
(to) **happen** случиться *sloocheet'sa;* **what has happened?** что случилось? *shto sloochilas'*
hard твёрдый *tvyordyi*
hard-boiled egg крутое яйцо *krootoye iitso*
hare заяц *zayats*
hat шапка *shapka*
(to) **have** иметь *imyet';* **I have** у меня есть *oo minya yest'*
hazel nut орехи *aryekhi*
(to) **heat** разогревать *razagryevat'*
heating отопление *ataplyenye*
heavy тяжёлый *tyazholyi*

hello! bye-bye! привет *privyet*
(to) **help** помогать *pamagat'*
here здесь *zdyes'*
herring сельдь *syel't'*
high chair кресло *kryesla*
hire прокат *prakat*
(to) **hold** держать *dirzhat'*
holiday праздник *praznik*
Holland Голландия *galandya*
honey мёд *myot*
hospital больница *bal'neetsa*
hot (peppery) острый *ostryi*
hot тёплый *tioplyi;* **(of food)** горячий *garyachii*
hotel гостиница *gasteenitsa*
hour час *chas*
house, home дом *dom*
housewife домашняя хозяйка *damashnyaya keh-zeeah-ee-kah*
how much сколько *skol'ka*
how как *kak*
hundred сто *sto*
hunger голод *golat*
hurry спешка *spyeshka;* **to be in a hurry** спешить *spisheet';* **to hurry** делать в спешке *dyelat' fspyeshki*
husband муж *moosh*
ice лёд *lyot*
ice-cream parlor кафе-мороженое *kafe marozhinaye*
ice-cream мороженое *marozhinaye*
identical одинаковый *adinakavyi*
ill больной *bal'noi*
illness болезнь *balyezn'*
immediately сразу *srazoo*
important важный *vazhnyi*
impossible невозможный *nivazmozhnyi*
in front of перед *pyerit*
in(side) внутри *vnootree*
included включённый *fklyoochonyi*
(to) **inform** информировать *infarmeeravat'*
information информация *infarmatsya*
infusion отвар *atvar*
inn трактир *trakteer*
innocuous безвредный *bizvryednyi*
insect насекомое *nasikomaye*
instead напротив *naprotif*
integral полный *polnyi*
interesting интересный *intiryesnyi*

internal внутренний *vnootrinii*
(to) **invite** приглашать *priglashat'*
invoice фактура *faktoora*
Ireland Ирландия *irlandya*
iron (for clothes) утюг *ootyook*
Italian итальянец/итальянка *m or f noun ital'yanits/ital'yanka; adj* итальянский *italyanskii*
Italy Италия *italya*

jacket пиджак *pidzhak*
jam варенье *varyenye*
jam конфитюр *kanfityoor*
January январь *yenvar'*
jug кувшин *koofsheen*
juice (from meat) подливка *padleefka*
juice сок *sok*
July июль *yool'*
June июнь *yoon'*
juniper можжевельник *mazhivyel'nik*
just *adv* именно *eemina*

(to) **keep** беречь *biryech'*
kid (young goat) козлёнок *kazlionak*
kitchen garden огород *agarot*
kitchen кухня *kookhnya*
kiwi киви *keevi*
knife нож *nosh*
(to) **know** знать *znat'*

label этикетка *etikyetka*
lake озеро *ozira*
lamb молочный барашек *malochnii barashik*
lamb ягнёнок *yagnyonak*
lard шпик *shpeek*
large большой *bal'shoi*
last последний *paslyednii*
(to) **leave** *astavlyat'*
(to) **leave** (depart) уехать *ooyekhat'*
leek лук-порей *look paryei*
leg нога *naga*
lemon лимон *limon*
lemonade лимонад *limanat*
lens линза *leenza;* **contact lenses** контактные линзы *kantaktnyi leenzi*
lentils чечевица *chicheevitsa*
less меньше *myen'she*
lettuce латук *latook*
life жиознь *zhizn'*
lift лифт *lift*
(to) **light** включать *fklyoochat'*

light свет *svyet*
light лёгкий *lyokhkii*
(to) **like: I like milk** мне нравится молоко *mnye nravitsa malako*
line линия *leenya*
liqueur ликёр *likyor*
liquid *adj* жидкий *zheetkii*
list список *speesak;* **telephone directory** телефонная книга *tilifonaya kneega*
lit включённый *fklyoochonyi*
liter литр *leetr*
little мало *mala*
(to) **live** жить *zheet'*
liver печень *pyechin'*
lobster омар *amar*
local местный *myestnyi*
long длинный *dleenyi*
(to) **look** смотреть *smatryet'*
(to) **lose** потерять *patirytat'*
luce щука *shooka*

mackerel скумбрия *skoombria*
maize cob початок *pachatak*
maize кукуруза *kookoorooza*
marjoram майоран *maioran*
management дирекция *diryektsia*
manager директор *diryektar*
mandarin мандарин *mandareen*
map карта *karta*
March март *mart*
marinated маринад *marinat*
market рынок *reenak*
match спичка *speechka*
May май *mai*
mayonnaise майонез *mayanes*
meal еда *yeda*
(to) **mean** значить *znachit';* **what does it mean?** что значит? *shto znachit?*
measure размер *rasmyer*
meat мясо *myasa;* **tinned meat** мясные консервы *miasnyi kansiervi;* **mince** фарш *farsh*
meatballs биточки *bitochki*
medicine медицина *miditseena*
(to) **meet** встречать *fstryechat'*
melon дыня *deenya*
menu меню *minyoo*
meringue безе *byeze*
Milan Милан *milan*
milk shake молочный

коктейль *malochnyi kakteil'*
milk молоко *malako*
(to) **mince** нашинковать *nashinkavat'*
mince (meat) мелко рубленый *myelka rooblinyi*
mint мята *myata*
minute минута *minoota*
mistake ошибка *asheepka*
misunderstanding недоразумение *nedarazoomyenye*
mixed смешанный *smyesshanyi*
mixture смесь *smyes'*
mollusks моллюски *malyooski*
Monday понедельник *panidyel'nik*
month месяц *myesiats*
monuments памятники *pamyatniki*
moon луна *loona*
more больше *bol'she*
morning утро *ootra*
Moscow Москва *maskva*
mosquitoes комары *kamaree*
mother мать *mat'*
mouth рот *rot*
Mr, gentleman господин *gaspadeen*
Mrs, lady госпожа *gaspazha*
much очень *ocheen'*
mullet кефаль *kyefal'*
museum музей *moozei*
mushrooms грибы *gribee*; **fresh mushrooms** свежие грибы *svyezhii gribee*; **dried mushrooms** сушёные грибы *sooshonyi gribee*
music музыка *moozyka*
mussels мидии *meedii*
mustard горчица *garcheetsa*

nails опята *apyata*
name имя *eemya*
Naples Неаполь *nyapal'*
narrow узкий *ooskii*
nation страна *strana*
near *adv* близко *bleeska*
need нужда *noozhda*; **I need** мне нужно *mnye noozhna*
never никогда *nikagda*
New Year Новый год *novyi got*
new новый *novyi*
newspaper газета *gazyeta*
night ночь *noch*
no нет *nyet*
nobody никто *nikto*
noise шум *shoom*
noisy шумный *shoomnyi*

non-alcoholic безалкогольный *bizalkagol'nyi*
non-smoker некурящий *nikooryashii*
north север *syevyer*
not не *nye*
nothing ничего *nichivo*
November ноябрь *nayabr'*
number номер *nomyer*
nut грецкий орех *gryetskii aryekh;* **coconut** кокосовый орех *kakosavyi aryekh;* **nutmeg** мускатный орех *mooskatnyi aryekh*
nutcracker щипцы для орехов *shiptsi dlya aryekhaf*

oat овёс *avyos*
(to) **obtain** получать *paloochat'*
occupied занятый *zanyatyi*
October октябрь *aktyabr'*
octopus полип *paleep*
often часто *chasta*
oil растительное масло *rasteetel'naye masla*
old старый *staryi*
olive оливки *aleefki;* **black olives** чёрные оливки *chornyi aleefki;* **green olives** зелёные оливки *zilyonyi aleefki*
omelette омлет *amlyet*
omelette яичница *iishnitsa*
on на *na*
onion лук *look*
only только *tol'ka*
(to) **open (a bottle)** откупорить *atkooporit'*
open открыто *atkreeta;* **outside** на открытом воздухе *na atkreetam vosdookhi*
orange апельсин *apil'seen*
orangeade апельсиновый напиток *apil'seenavyi napeetak*
(to) **order** заказать *zakazat'*
order заказ *zakas*
other другой *droogoi*
outside снаружи *snaroozhi*
oven печь *pyech'*
owner хозяин *khazyain*
ox вол *vol*
oysters устрицы *oostritsi*

pain, ache боль *bol';* **stomach ache** боль в животе *bol' vzhivatye* **or** боль в желудке *bol' vzhilootkye;* **headache** головная боль *galavnaya bol'*

pair пара *para*
pan кастрюля *kastryoolya*
paper handkerchief бумажный платок *boomazhnyi platok*
parents родители *radeetili*
park парк *park*
parmesan пармезан *parmizan*
parsley петрушка *pyetrooshka*
part часть *chast'*
passport паспорт *paspart*
paté паштет *pashtyet*
(to) **pay** платить *platit'*
payment оплата *aplata*
peanut арахис *arakhis*
pear груша *groosha*
peas зелёный горошек *zilyonyi garoshek*
(to) **peel** чистить *cheestit'*
peel корка *korka*
pencil карандаш *karandash*
pepper чёрный перец *chornyi pyerits*
peppers стручковый перец *stroochkovyi pyerits*
perch окунь *okkoon'*
perhaps может быть *mozhet beet'*
permit разрешение *razrishenye*
persimmon хурма *khoorma*
pharmacy аптека *aptyeka*
pheasant фазан *fazan*
phone call звонок *zanok*
photograph фотография *fotografya*
pickles маринованные овощи *miree-novanyi ovashi*
pie пирог *pirok;* запеканка *zapikanka*
piece кусок *koosok*
pig свинья *svinya;* **pork** свинина *svineena*
pigeon голубь *goloop'*
pill пилюля *pilyoolya*
pin брошь *brosh;* **safety pin** булавка *boolafka*
pine nuts кедровые орехи *kyedravyi aryekhi*
pineapple ананас *ananas*
pink розовый *rozavyi*
pistachio nuts фисташки *fistashki*
place место *myesta*
plane самолёт *samalyot*
(to) **play (a game)** играть *igrat'*
please пожалуйста *pazhalsta*
pleased довольный *davol'nyi*
pleasure удовольствие *oodavol'stvye*

plums сливы *sleevi*
police милиция *mileetsyia*
pork свинина *svineena*
portion порция *portsya*
possible возможный *vazmozhnyi*
post office почта *pochta*
postcard открытка *atkreetka*
potatoes картофель *kartofyel'*; **fried potatoes** жареный картофель *zharinyi kartofyel'*; **boiled potatoes** варёный картофель *varyonyi kartofyel'*
power власть *vlast'*
(to) **prefer** предпочитать *pryetpachitat'*
pregnant беременная *biryeminaya*
(to) **prepare** готовить *gatovit'*
(to) **preserve** хранить *khraneet'*
preserved in oil в масле *vmasli*
preserved meats колбасные изделия *kalbasnye izdyelya*
preserves консервированный *kansirveeravanyi*
price цена *tsina*
private частный *chastnyi*
products товары *tavari*
pudding пудинг *poodink*
pulses бобовые *babovyi*
pumpkin тыква *teekva*
purée пюре *poore*; **vegetable purée** протёртые овощи *pratyortyi ovaschi*
purée пюре *pyooré*
purse сумочка *soomachka*
(to) **put** положить *palazheet'*

quail перепел *pyeripil*
quarter четвёртый *chitvyortyi*
question вопрос *vapros*
quiet ровный *rovnyi*

rabbit кролик *krolik*
radio радио *radio*
radish редиска *rideeska*
ragout соус *sowoos*
rain дождь *dosht*
raincoat плащ *plash*
raisins изюм *izyoom*
raspberries малина *maleena*
raw сырой *seeroi*
(to) **read** читать *chitat'*
ready готовый *gatovyi*
receipt расписка *raspeeska*
recipe рецепт *ritsept*

red mullet краснобородка *krasnabarotka*
red красный *krasnyi*
refrigerator холодильник *khaladeel'nik*
refund возмещение *vazmishenye*
region область *oblast'*
(to) **remove the fat** снимать жир *snimat' zhir*
(to) **repeat** повторять *paftaryat'*
(to) **reserve** забронировать *zabraneeravat'*
reserved забронированный *zabraneeravanyi*
restaurant ресторан *ristaran*
(to) **return** вернуться *virnoot'sa*
return возвращение *vazvrarshenye*
rhubarb ревень *rivyen'*
rice рис *rees*
right правая сторона *pravaya starana;* **to the right** справа *sprava*
right *noun* право *prava*
ring cake кекс *keks*
ripe зрелый *zryelyi*
river река *rika*
road дорога *daroga*
roast ростбиф *rostbif*
roasted жареный *zharinyi*
roll бутерброд *booterbrot*
room комната *komnata;* **hotel room** номер *nomir* **hall** зал *zal;* **dining room** столовая *stalovaya*
rosé розовый *rozavyi*
rosemary розмарин *razmareen*
rubber резина *rizeena;* **chewing gum** жвачка *zhvachka*
rum ром *rom*
Russia Россия *raseeia*
Russian русский *rooskii*
rustic сельский *syel'skii*

saffron шафран *shafran*
sage сальвия *sal'vya*
Saint Petersburg Петербург *peterboork*
salad салат *salat*
salmon лосось *lasos';* сёмга *syomga*
salt соль *sol'*
salt-cellar солонка *salonka*
same тот же *totzhe*
sandwich сандвич *sandvich*
sardines сардины *sardeeni*
Saturday суббота *soobota*
sauce соус *sowoos*
saucepan кастрюля *kastryoolya*
sausage сарделька *sardyel'ka*

savory biscuits солёное печенье *salyonaye pichenye*
savory солёный *salyonyi*
(to) **say,** (to) **tell** говорить *gavareet'*
scampi омары *amari*
sea food дары моря *daree morya*
sea море ***mo**rye*
season сезон *sizon*
second второй *ftaroi*
(to) **see** видеть *vidyet'*
(to) **sell** продавать *pradavat'*
semolina манная каша *manaya kasha*
September сентябрь *sintyabr'*
service обслуживание *apsloozhivanye*
(to) **set** накрыть *nakreet'*
(to) **shell** очищать от скорлупы *achishat' atskarloopee*
shell скорлупа *skarloopa*
shell ракушка *rakooshka*
sherry херес *khyeres*
ship корабль *karabl'*
shirt рубашка *roobashka*
shoes ботинки *bateenki*
shop магазин *magazeen*
shopping покупки *pakoopki*
shoulder плечо *plicho*
(to) **show** показать *pakazat'*
show спектакль *spiktakl'*
shrimps креветки *krivyetki*
Sicily Сицилия *sitseelya*
side-dish гарнир *garneer*
sight вид *veet*
signature подпись *potpis'*
simple простой *prastoi*
sirloin филе из говядины *filye izgavyadini*
skin кожа *kozha*
(to) **sleep** спать *spat'*
slice (of meat) ломтик мясо *lomtik myasa*
slice кусок *koosok*
sliced bread тостер *toster*
sliced meats колбасные изделия *kalbasnyi izdyelii*
small cake пирожное *pirozhnaye*
small change мелочь *myelach*
small glass рюмка *ryoomka*
small маленький *malyen'kii*
smell запах *zapakh*
(to) **smoke** курить *kooreet'*
smoke дым *deem*
smoked копчёный *kapchonyi*
smoker курящий *kooryashii*
smoking *adj* дымящийся *deemyaschiisya*
smooth ровный *rovnyi*

snack bar бистро *bistro*
snack закуска *zakooska*
snails улитки *ooleetki*
soap мыло *meela*
sole (fish) камбала *kambala*
some какой-то *kakoita*
some, any несколько *nyeskal'ka*
someone кто-то *ktota*
something что-то *shtota*
son сын *seen*
song песня *pyesnya*
soup суп *soop*
sour cherry вишня *vishnya*
sour кислый *keeslyi*
south юг *yook*
South America Южная Америка *ioozhnaya amyerika*
soya соя *soya*
sparkling шипучий *sheepoochii*
(to) **speak** говорить *gavareet'*
spices приправы *pripravi*
spinach шпинат *shpinat*
spit вертел *vyertil*
spoon ложка *lushka*
spring cabbage капуста *kapoosta*
square (in a town) площадь *ploshat*
stairs лестница *lyesnitsa*
stamp марка *marka*
starch крахмал *krakhmal*
(to) **start** начать *nachat'*
starter закуска *zakooska*
station вокзал *vagzal*
(to) **stay** оставаться *astavat'sa*
steak бифштекс *bifshteks*
steam пар *par*
stew *noun* жаркое *zharkoye*
stewed, braised тушёный *tooshonyi*
sticking plaster пластырь *plasteer'*
stomach желудок *zhiloodak*
(to) **stop** остановить *astanaveet'*
stop остановка *astanofka;* **bus-stop** остановка автобуса *astanofka aftoboosa;* **subway stop** станция метро *stantsya mitro*
strawberry клубника *kloobneeka*
street улица *oolitsa*
strong сильный *seelnyi;* **(of wine)** крепкий *kryepkii*
stuffed фаршированный *faschirovanyi*
stuffing начинка *nacheenka*
subway метро *mitro*

sugar bowl сахарница *sakharnitsa*
sugar сахар *sakhar*
suitcase чемодан *chimadan*
summer *adj* летний *lyetnii*
summer *noun* лето *lyeta*
summer berries лесные ягоды *lesneei iagady*
Sunday воскресенье *vaskrisyenye*
superalcoholic drinks крепкие алкогольные напитки *kryepkii alkagol'nyi napeetki*
supper ужин *oozhin*
surname фамилия *fameelya*
sweet (wine) полусладкое *palooslatkaye*
sweet *adj* сладкий *slatkii; noun* сладкое *slatkaye*
sweet-and-sour кислосладкий *keslaslatkii*
sweets сладости *sladasti*
(to) **swim** плавать *plavat'*
swimming pool бассейн *basein*
(to) **switch off** выключать *viklyoochat'*
Switzerland Швейцария *shvitsarya*
swordfish рыба-мечь *reebamyech*
syrup сироп *sirop*
table cloth скатерть *skatirt'*
table стол *stol*
table napkin салфетка *salfyetka*
tablet таблетка *tablyetka*
talcum powder тальк *tal'k*
(to) **take** взять *vzyat'*
(to) **take off/away** снимать *snimat'*
tap кран *kran*
(to) **taste** пробовать *probavat'*
taste вкус *fkoos*
taste проба *proba*
tasty вкусный *fkoosnyi*
tavern трактир *trakteer*
taxi такси *taksee*
tea чай *chai*
teaspoon ложечка *lozhichka*
telegram телеграмма *tiligrama*
telephone телефон *tilifon*
temperature температура *timpiratoora;* **room temperature** комнатная температура *komnatnaya timpiratoora*
tender нежный *nyezhnyi*
terminus конечная *kanyechnaya*
terrace терраса *tirasa*
thank you спасибо *spaseeba*

(to) **thank** благодарить *blagadareet'*
that тот *tot*
that, which что *shto*
then потом *patom*
there там *tam*
thigh ляжка *lyashka;* **drumstick** куриная ножка *kooreenaya noshka*
thin тонкий *tonkii*
thin худой *khoodoi;* **(of a dish)** нежирный *nizheernyi*
thing вещь *vyesh'*
third третий *tryetii*
thirst жажда *zhazhda*
this этот *etat*
this evening сегодня вечером *sivodnya vyechiram*
thousand тысяча *teesiacha*
thread нить *neet'*
throat горло *gohrla*
(to) **throw** бросать *brosat'*
Thursday четверг *chitvyerk*
thyme тимьян *timyan*
ticket билет *bilyet*
tie галстук *galstook*
time время *vryemya*
timetable расписание *raspisanye*
tip чаевые *chayeveeye*
toast (to your health) тост *tost*
toasted поджаренный *padzharinyi*
tobacco табак *tabak*
tobacconist's табакерка *tabakyerka*
today сегодня *sivodnya*
together вместе *vmyesti*
toilet туалет *tualyet*
tomato помидор *pamidor*
tomorrow завтра *zaftra*
tongue, language язык *iazeek*
too much слишком *sleeshkam*
tooth зуб *zoop*
toothpaste зубная паста *zoobnaya pasta*
toothpicks зубочистка *zoobacheeska*
towards в отношении *vatnashenii; (direction)* к *k*
towel полотенце *palatyentse*
train поезд *poist*
tranquillizer успокойтзлвноз *oospakaeetil'naye*
transport транспорт *transpart;* **means of transport** виды

транспорта *veedy transparta*
(to) **travel** путешествовать *pootishestvovat'*
tray поднос *padnos*
trip поездка *payestka*
tripe рубец *roobyets*
trolley тележка *tilyeshka*
trout форель *farel'*
truffles трюфель *tryoofyel'*
trunk call междугородний звонок *mizhdoogarodnyi zvanok*
(to) **try** пробовать *probavat'*
Tuesday вторник *ftornik*
tuna тунец *tunyets*
turbot палтус *paltoos*
tureen глиняная миска *gleenianya meeska*
Turin Турин *tooreen*
turkey индюшка *indyooshka*
(to) **turn** вращать *vrashat'*
turn *noun* **(of a spit)** оборот *abarot*
turnip репа *ryepa*
type род *rot*

ugly некрасивый *nikraseevyi*
umbrella зонт *zont*
uncomfortable неудобный *nyoodobnyi*
under под *pot*
underdone кровью *skrovyoo*
United States Соединённые Штаты *saidinyonyi shtati*
(to) **understand** понимать *panimat'*
until до *da*
(to) **use** использовать *ispol'zavat'*

vanilla ваниль *vaneel'*
VAT налог на добавленную стоимость *nalok na dabavlinooyoo stoimast'*
veal телятина *tilyatina*
vegetables овощи *ovashi*
vegetarian вегетарианский *vigitaryanskii*
Venice Венеция *vinyetsia*
vinegar уксус *ooksoos*
vintage год *got*
vitamins витаминны *vitameeni*
vodka водка *votka*

(to) **wait** ждать *zhdat'*
waiter официант *afitsiant*
waitress официантка *afitsyantka*
wall стена *stina*
wallet бумажник *boomazhnik*

(to) **walk** ходить *khadeet'*
(to) **want** хотеть *khatyet'*
(to) **wash** мыть *meet'*
wasp оса *asa*
watch часы *chasee*
water вода *vada;* **mineral water** минеральная вода *miniral'naia vada;* **natural water** натуральная вода *natural'naia vada;* **sparkling water** газированная вода *gazirovanaia vada*
water melon арбуз *arboos*
way способ *sposap*
weak слабый *slabyi*
weather погода *pagoda*
Wednesday среда *srida*
week неделя *nidyelya*
weekday будний *boodnii*
weight вес *vyes*
welcome добро пожаловать *dabro pazhalavat'*
well хорошо *kharasho*
west запад *zapat*
what? что? *shto?*
when когда *kagda*
where где *gdye*
which какой *kakoi*
while когда *kagda*
(to) **whisk** взбивать *vzbivat'*
white белый *byelyi*
whiting мерлан *mirlan*
who кто *kto*
whole целый *tselyi*
why почему *pachimoo*
wife жена *zhina*
window окно *akno*
wine вино *vino;* **white wine** белое вино *byelaye vino;* **red wine** красное вино *krasnaye vino;* **rosé** розовое вино *rozavaye vino;* **light wine** лёгкое вино *liokhkaye vino;* **fortified wine** креплёное вино *kryeplyonaye vino*
winter зима *zima*
with breadcrumbs панированный *panirovanyi*
with с *s*
with syrup в сиропе *fsiropye*
without без *byes*
woman женщина *zhenshina*
wood дерево *dyeriva*
word слово *slova*
(to) **work** работать *rabotat'*
work работа *rabota*
would like хотеть *khatyet'*
wrapped упакованный *oopakovanyi*
(to) **write** писать *pisat'*
wurstel сосиски *saseeski*

year год *got*
yeast дрожжи *drozhzhi*
yellow жёлтый *zholtyi*
yesterday вчера *fchira*
yogurt йогурт *iogoort*
yolk желток *zhiltok*
young cockerel цыплёнок *tsiplyonak*
young lady девушка *dyevooshka*
young man молодой человек *maladoi chilavyek*
young молодой *maladoi*

zucchini кабачки *kabachkee*

INDEX

In the same series:

How to Eat Out in Italy
How to Eat Out in France
How to Eat Out in Spain
How to Eat Out in Russia
How to Eat Out in Greece
How to Eat Out in Portugal & Brazil